"I do not know a more reliable guide to biblical worship than Derek Thomas, a friend and former colleague who has taught me so much over the years. This book epitomizes his writings—rich, yet readable. Practical, but full of biblical and theological insight. I plan to recommend this book to anyone who wants to know why we at our church are committed to historic, Reformed worship."

—DR. WILLIAM BARCLEY
Senior pastor, Sovereign Grace Presbyterian Church
Charlotte, N.C.

"John Calvin said, 'The first foundation of righteousness is the worship of God.' While each Reformed denomination has its particular manner of worship with regard to various details, Derek Thomas offers a lively introduction to several principles and practices of classic Reformed worship. This book will prove very helpful to church members and visitors."

—DR. JOEL R. BEEKE
President, Puritan Reformed Theological Seminary
Grand Rapids, Mich.

"Derek Thomas writes to an important audience: traditional churches whose members don't know why they worship as they do, and new members of traditional churches who don't know why their newfound church home worships as it does. Thomas provides a brief but comprehensive explanation of historic Reformed worship, beginning with the doctrine of the church, the role of the Christian Sabbath, and the regulative principle. He then provides a guided tour through each element of worship from the reading and preaching of God's Word, to the collection, to prayer, to creeds, to sung praises, to the administration of the sacraments, and finally to the benediction. For those looking for a succinct explanation of historic Reformed worship, here is a guide that you can place in the hands of inquirers, whether they've been sitting in the pews for decades or are newly arrived."

—Dr. Terry Johnson
Senior minister, Independent Presbyterian Church
Savannah, Ga.

"God is to be praised as Creator, Redeemer and Sustainer. So why did God create us? To the praise of His glory. Why does He save us? To the praise of His glorious grace. Why does God providentially sustain us? 'Let everything that has breath praise the Lord!' Derek Thomas has provided for us a biblical and focused, straightforward distillation of the primacy of God-centered, Spirit-filled, Christ-exalting, biblically revealed, and gospel-saturated worship that is pleasing to the One who created, saved, and sustains us so that we may give the triune God true worship. The God of glory is to be worshiped rightly in Spirit and truth. This volume is a page-turner for all who once fell short of His glory and now have no greater desire than to give Him glory when gathered with His people and when scattered to exalt Him in all of life.

—Dr. Harry Reeder III
Senior pastor, Briarwood Presbyterian Church
Birmingham, Ala.

Let Us Worship God

Let Us Worship God

Why We Worship the Way We Do

DEREK W.H. THOMAS

 LIGONIER MINISTRIES

Let Us Worship God: Why We Worship the Way We Do
© 2021 by Derek W.H. Thomas

Published by Ligonier Ministries
421 Ligonier Court, Sanford, FL 32771
Ligonier.org

Printed in Ann Arbor, Michigan
Cushing-Malloy, Inc.
0000821
First edition

ISBN 978-1-64289-356-4 (Paperback)
ISBN 978-1-64289-357-1 (ePub)
ISBN 978-1-64289-358-8 (Kindle)

Cover design: Metaleap Creative
Interior design and typeset: Katherine Lloyd/The DESK

Unless otherwise noted, Scripture quotations are from the ESV® Bible (The Holy Bible, English Standard Version®), copyright © 2001 by Crossway, a publishing ministry of Good News Publishers. Used by permission. All rights reserved.

Scripture quotations marked KJV are from the King James Version. Public domain.

Library of Congress Control Number: 2021932198

To

the members and friends

of First Presbyterian Church,

Columbia, South Carolina,

and

Dr. David Lockington

Contents

Preface

"Let us worship God!"

Whenever I say these words on a Sunday morning, something supernatural occurs. In Jesus' own words: "For where two or three are gathered in my name, there am I among them" (Matt. 18:20). Think of it! Jesus comes and joins in our worship. He brings us His Word, His promise, His encouragement. He sings with us (Heb. 2:12). How vital, therefore, that we worship in a manner He prescribes!

These pages arose out of a need to explain to my congregation (First Presbyterian Church, Columbia, S.C.) why it is that we worship the way we do. First Presbyterian is more than 225 years old, and in its long and profound history, it has maintained a manner of worship that today we would refer to as "historic" or "classical." While we easily grow accustomed to doing things a certain way and therefore refer to it as "traditional," new members (who join because of the preaching more than any other factor) often ask why we do or don't do such and such. Typically, I address this in the inquirers class that is designed for new members. But I also became aware that while no discontent was evident among long-standing members, there was little by way of a theological understanding as to why we worship in the manner that we do. Hence, I preached a series of sermons that formed the substance of these pages. Sermons and books are very different things, and these pages are weightier than the sermons that underpin them.

Initially, I thought of writing this book simply for our own members, but I have been persuaded that its contents will have value beyond our own church. I have tried not to be overly critical of other traditions. My aim was a more positive one: to provide theological and scriptural support for the liturgical aspects of our corporate worship.

The sermons were preached before the pandemic of 2020, but the book was largely assembled during the chaos that COVID-19 brought upon the church worldwide. At one point, gathered, in-person worship ceased for fifteen weeks and we learned the value of livestreaming. Even now, as I write these words, only 35 percent of our typical attendance has returned. We have learned the blessings and curses of Zoom! But one vital lesson has emerged: gathered worship on the Lord's Day is a vital part of our Christian life. We have renewed empathy for our brothers and sisters who live in parts of the world where gathered worship may cost them their lives and for whom our experience in 2020 was a very small window into what they experience all their lives.

There are many people to thank, not least my dear friends who encouraged me to write this book, especially my colleague in preaching, Dr. Gabe Fluhrer, whose constant words of encouragement to write have been a source of great comfort. I am also thankful for Bill and Nancy Neely, whose generosity in allowing me to stay in their beach home in Litchfield, S.C., while writing the final pages of this book proved a little taste of heaven. I am also blessed to have an exceptionally smart intern, Beck Otersen, and his savvy work is evident in the formatting of many of the footnotes. Most of all, I am grateful to my long-suffering wife, Rosemary, without whom not a word of it would have been written. As we traverse our fifth decade of marriage together, I am more grateful each day for the bride the Lord gave me.

This book was written with the wonderful congregation of First Presbyterian Church, Columbia, S.C., in mind. It has been the greatest privilege of my ministry to serve the church as their senior minister. I dedicate this book to all the members and friends of this extraordinary church and count myself blessed to know and serve them.

I also want to dedicate it to my wonderful son-in-law, David Lockington, and ask his forgiveness for the chapter about inclusive, accompanied psalm singing! (He will understand.) I cannot imagine a better father to my two grandchildren, and I count it a blessed day when my daughter introduced him to us two decades ago.

Now, turn the page and start reading. I hope this book will make your Sunday worship even more meaningful.

Derek W.H. Thomas
October 2020

1

The *Local Church*

Jesus only has one plan, and it's called *church*! "I will build my church" (Matt. 16:18).

The author of Hebrews exhorts his readers, "And let us consider how to stir up one another to love and good works, not neglecting to meet together, as is the habit of some, but encouraging one another, and all the more as you see the Day drawing near" (Heb. 10:24–25).

Christians are meant to assemble together, especially on the Lord's Day. They are meant to worship *together*. Theologians speak of the "visible" church: the church that is made up of all those who profess to be Christians. Paedobaptists include children in this definition. The point is its *visibility*. It is not a secret society. It has a certain structure. It is made up of people who believe certain truths and live out a certain lifestyle. They do things together in a manner that is purposeful and sets them apart. And one important reason for a visible assembling of God's people is to worship God in a manner prescribed by Scripture.

During the COVID-19 pandemic of 2020 when churches across the entire world "shut down," they didn't cease to be visible churches. Churches are not defined by buildings. Meeting online may be irregular, but it is not illegal. The author of Hebrews hardly envisaged the internet, but virtual worship in seasons of extremity do meet many of the objectives of worship.

The purpose of this book is to examine the nature of this collective, corporate worship. The church exists for other purposes—to evangelize or provide service in and for the community, for example. But its primary purpose is to worship the true and living God.

The New Testament church emerged as a consequence of the death and resurrection of Jesus. Some speculate as to whether Jesus intended to create a visible church, but that seems totally contrary to Scripture, especially to the words of Jesus.

A key text is Matthew 16:13–20. Jesus and the disciples were in Caesarea Philippi and were discussing what people were saying about His identity. Some thought He was John the Baptist raised from the dead. Others opined that He may be Elijah, or Jeremiah, or one of the prophets. And then Peter had a defining moment in which he confessed Jesus to be the "Christ, the Son of the living God." It is clear that the confession arose due to a revelation given to him by the Father in heaven. Playing on the similarity of Peter's name and the Greek word for "rock," Jesus responded: "And I tell you, you are Peter, and on this rock I will build my church, and the gates of hell shall not prevail against it. I will give you the keys of the kingdom of heaven, and whatever you bind on earth shall be bound in heaven, and whatever you loose on earth shall be loosed in heaven" (vv. 18–19). Several issues need underlining.

First, without getting embroiled in fanciful Roman Catholic claims that Peter is the first pope, it is clear that Peter is being given a primary role in the establishment of the New Testament church. The first section of the book of Acts is about Peter's role after Pentecost while Paul is still a hostile Jewish assassin. Peter—broken and fragile as he was—is the one Jesus chooses. That in itself should encourage us.

Second, Jesus refers to the church as "*my* church." Pastors frequently talk about their churches, often to boast about the size of the membership or the budget. In doing so, they often use the words "my church is . . ." But it is not "my" church; it is Jesus' church. He is King and Head of the church. "And he put all things under his feet and gave him as head over all things to the church, which is his body, the fullness of him who fills all in all" (Eph. 1:22–23). As Lord of the church, Jesus alone dictates what the church does. He establishes the program. He sets the agenda. And, as we shall see, this is vitally important when answering the question, *How* should we worship?

Third, this is the first time Jesus employs the word "church" (Greek *ekklēsia*). Up to this point, Jesus spoke about "kingdom" ("the kingdom of God" or, especially in Matthew, "the kingdom of heaven"), but never once had He talked about "church." And yet, none of the disciples asked Him what the word meant! Obviously, they had some basic understanding of the word. And, by the time Matthew wrote his gospel a generation later, his readers knew all too well what the word meant, and therefore Matthew does not stop to give an explanation. The word *ekklēsia* is the Greek translation of the Hebrew word for "assembly" or "congregation" (*qahal*) in the Greek version of the Old Testament, known as the Septuagint (or LXX, the Roman numerals for seventy after the tradition that seventy Jewish rabbis were involved in its translation). The word *qahal* suggests a people "called" together for the purpose of communion with God.

The same idea of gathering lies behind the term *synagogue*. Jesus was telling Peter that His people will meet together in fellowship with God and in fellowship with one another. And, as Peter will go on to interpret, Christians belong to a community that is "called ... out of darkness into his marvelous light" (1 Peter 2:9). The church exists in the world and has responsibilities to the world, but it is also fundamentally *separate from* the world. She breathes a different atmosphere from that of the fallen world in which she lives. The church, as Jesus reminds us in His High Priestly Prayer, is *in* the world but not *of* the world (John 17:14–15). This leads to another conclusion suggested in Jesus' words to Peter.

Fourth, the church can expect opposition. In this instance, it is the opposition of "the gates of hell." Satan and his demons will attempt at every stage to destroy the church. Through difficulty, division, and discouragement, the warriors from hell will attempt to destroy what Christ has established. There will be seasons of assault ("the evil day," Eph. 6:13), but they will not ultimately prevail. The term "gates of hell" (Greek *pulai hadou*) is an Old Testament term meaning "death." The Septuagint translation of Job 38:17, for example, reads, "Have the gates of death been revealed to you, or have you seen the gates of deep darkness [*puloroi de hadou*]?" What Jesus is saying is that the church will not be destroyed by death. On the contrary, at death Christ's people will join the *invisible* church in heaven.

Pentecost and Beyond

Seven weeks after the resurrection of Christ, Peter stood in Jerusalem and declared that the ancient prophecies of the coming of the Holy Spirit were now fulfilled (Acts 2:14–41; see Joel 2:28–32; Isa. 32:15, 44; Ezek. 36:27). God's Spirit was poured forth and three thousand people believed Peter's message. The church as we know it began. Well, not exactly. There were no buildings that looked like churches—a reminder that the church is not a building even though we fairly consistently use the word to mean just that (one of the reasons that the Puritans referred to the building as a meeting house, and it would spare a great deal of confusion if we returned to the practice).

The book of Acts tells the story of the growth of the New Testament church. It has to navigate the difficult issue of Jewish-gentile relationships. We see the election of what looks like proto-deacons to provide care for Hellenistic and Jewish widows (Acts 6:1–7). And, as persecution erupts in Jerusalem, and Christians flee north and west, we see friction in Antioch when Peter and Paul come to verbal blows over fellowship with gentiles (Gal. 2:11–14). Through Paul's increasing influence and priority over Peter, churches were established in places like Galatia, Thessalonica, Ephesus, and Corinth. Rome is the exception in that the church there seems to have come into being largely through Christians moving there rather than by an Apostolic presence. At the end of Acts, the gospel has reached almost the entire known world. Churches are now present in most of the major cities of the Roman Empire, in which Sunday worship is observed and prayer and preaching and singing are component parts of what they do.

The church grew and developed organizationally and structurally. There is, for example, the development of the notion of "office" ("deacons," 1 Tim. 3:8–13; "overseer," 1 Tim. 3:1–7 and Titus 1:7–9; "elders," Titus 1:5–9). And for the first three hundred years or so, the church met almost exclusively in people's homes (house churches) rather than in designated buildings. House churches are mentioned in the homes of Mary (John Mark's mother, Acts 12:12), Lydia (Acts 16:40), Prisca and Aquila (Rom. 16:3, 5), Nympha (Col. 4:15), and Philemon and Apphia (Philem. 1–2).

After Pentecost, a discernible pattern emerges that Luke summarizes this way: "They devoted themselves to the apostles' teaching and the fellowship, to the breaking of bread and the prayers" (Acts 2:42). We will take a look at this verse again later, but all these aspects of worship require meeting corporately. In our day, there is the phenomenon of "unchurched Christians," something for which the New Testament does not allow. Indeed, Cyprian, bishop of Carthage in the third century, famously coined the phrase *extra ecclesiam nulla salus*, meaning "outside the church there is no salvation." The phrase has been employed as part of the Roman Catholic dogma that those outside the formal boundaries of Roman Catholicism cannot be saved. However, this is not its intended meaning. The Westminster Confession of Faith, in a section on the church, added an extra word to clarify its intent: "out of which there is no *ordinary* possibility of salvation."[1] What the confession underlines is that usually Christians belong to a corporate body, the church. There are exceptions: "A repentant thief on the cross, a Muslim convert to Christianity who has not yet discovered other believers, or a man stranded on the desert island with only a Bible, each has plausible reasons for not being a part of a church."[2]

Jesus, but Not Church

There are siren voices in our time that suggest we can have Jesus but abandon the "institutional church." The mantra goes like this: "We want Jesus, or community, or discussion groups, or therapy, but not church." A forest of trees has been cut down to produce books with exotic titles like George Barna's *Revolution* and William P. Young's *The Shack*, both of which describe a churchless Christianity.[3] And then there are even more memorable titles like *Life after Church*, *Quitting Church*, and *So You Don't Want to Go to Church Anymore*.[4]

Finish the following sentences:

- "Church is so _____."
- "When I go to church, I want to be _____."
- "Church folk are so _____."
- "The worship style is so _____."

Let's be honest: the church can and does mess up. Churches get stuck in the past and mired in mindless routine. The worship can be stuffy or poorly done. And most of us have been in churches that appear unfriendly and unwelcoming.

People stop going to church and blame the church for it. They abandon church for a variety of reasons, and not all of them are good ones. Some churches, to be brutally honest, ought to be abandoned! No one should have to endure the pointlessness of a church that has abandoned the gospel. Such churches deserve no loyalty. Churches that violate clear and primary biblical expectations deserve to be closed. Not every church is a true, biblical church.

Scripture is very clear that a church displays certain "marks."[5] The Reformer Philip Melanchthon, in his *Loci Communes* (1543), wrote, "The marks which point out the pure church are the pure gospel and the proper use of the sacraments."[6] John Calvin also wrote something similar: "Wherever we see the Word of God purely preached and heard, and the sacraments administered according to Christ's institution, there, it is not to be doubted, a church of God exists."[7]

In addition to the preaching of the gospel and the right administration of the sacraments, the Belgic Confession added the administration of church discipline:

The true church can be recognized if it has the following marks: the church engages in the pure preaching of the gospel, it makes use of the pure administration of the sacraments as Christ instituted them, and it practices church discipline for correcting faults.

In short, it governs itself according to the pure Word of God, rejecting all things contrary to it and holding Jesus Christ as the only Head.[8]

Others have elaborated further requirements. John Stott, for example, identifies seven marks: "These then are the marks of the ideal Church—love, suffering, holiness, sound doctrine, genuineness, evangelism and humility. They are what Christ desires to find in His churches as He walks among them."[9] Mark Dever draws attention to *nine* marks: expositional preaching, biblical theology, the gospel, conversion, evangelism, church membership, church discipline, discipleship, and leadership.[10]

What Can We (Should We) Expect in a True Church?

So, we have joined a sound, biblical church. It isn't perfect, because nothing is perfect in this fallen world. When Christians gather, they bring remaining sin with them. Remaining sin in the lives of God's people often makes for considerable difficulty. But if not perfection, what reasonable expectations can we have? The author of Hebrews answers the question:

> Therefore, brothers, since we have confidence to enter the holy places by the blood of Jesus, by the new and living way that he opened for us through the curtain, that is, through his flesh, and since we have a great priest over the house of God, let us draw near with a true heart in full assurance of faith, with our hearts sprinkled clean from an evil conscience and our bodies washed with pure water. Let us hold fast the confession of our hope without

wavering, for he who promised is faithful. And let us consider how to stir up one another to love and good works, not neglecting to meet together, as is the habit of some, but encouraging one another, and all the more as you see the Day drawing near.

For if we go on sinning deliberately after receiving the knowledge of the truth, there no longer remains a sacrifice for sins, but a fearful expectation of judgment, and a fury of fire that will consume the adversaries. (Heb. 10:19–27)

There is more in these verses than we have space for in this chapter, but consider the following points.

First, there is the issue of *accountability*. This is what is implied in the suggestion that by assembling together, we have an opportunity to encourage one another. Why is this necessary? Because *not* assembling carries the very real threat of apostasy!

Can Christians commit apostasy? We need to be very clear about this question and what it is asking. The question is *not*, Can those who are regenerate lose their salvation? The answer to that is—*no*! Jesus gave a promise to that end: "I give them eternal life, and they will never perish, and no one will snatch them out of my hand. My Father, who has given them to me, is greater than all, and no one is able to snatch them out of the Father's hand" (John 10:28–29). Paul echoed a similar certainty when he wrote to the Philippians: "And I am sure of this, that he who began a good work in you will bring it to completion at the day of Jesus Christ" (Phil. 1:6).

But *professing* Christians do abandon the faith and die in unbelief. The New Testament refers to Christians in the same way we do—according to the phenomenon of their profession. We have no way of verifying their elect status. We cannot peer into the Lamb's

Book of Life and check if their names are there! All we can do is accept someone's *profession* of faith. But they may be a Judas. He too professed faith. They may be a Hymenaeus or Philetus who swerved from the truth (2 Tim. 2:17). They may be a Demas who fell in love with the world (2 Tim. 4:10).

Assembling together makes us accountable to one another. Our perseverance assumes our gathering together. The church has everything to do with our salvation. Paul writes to Timothy, "I am writing these things to you so that, if I delay, you may know how one ought to behave in the household of God, which is the church of the living God, a pillar and buttress of the truth" (1 Tim. 3:14–15). You will not be able to hold on to the truth if the church isn't a major part of your life.

Second, there is the issue of *strength*. According to the California Department of Parks and Recreation, California redwoods have shallow roots, no more than five to six feet deep. The redwoods (*Sequoia sempervirens*) can grow to 350 feet. "These trees have shallow root systems that extend over one hundred feet from the base, intertwining with the roots of other redwoods. This increases their stability during strong winds and floods."[11] There is strength in numbers.

It is what the Apostles' Creed means when it says, "I believe in *the communion of saints*." It is also, partly, what is meant in Acts 2:42 when Luke describes the post-Pentecost church as continuing in "fellowship." The word (Greek *koinōnia*) can also be rendered "participation" (cf. 1 Cor. 10:16, 18, 20). We share together certain beliefs, ambitions, material goods, and good works. We participate in life and worship *together*. We draw strength from one another.

Third, there is the issue of *purpose*. Hence the author of Hebrews urges, "Let us consider how to stir up one another to love and good works" (Heb. 10:24).

"Consider," the author of Hebrews writes. *Think about thinking!* The word suggests intense and thoughtful investigation. Christianity begins in the mind. It is vital to know what and why we believe something to be true. To cite the title of a book written by John Stott, *Your Mind Matters*.[12] The author of Hebrews used the word earlier in the epistle: "Therefore, holy brothers, you who share in a heavenly calling, *consider Jesus*" (Heb. 3:1, emphasis added). Set your minds to ponder who Jesus is and why He came and what He did and how you should respond to Him. The tense in Hebrews 10:24 suggests constant and repeated action: let us constantly consider one another.

The ability to stream worship services is a wonderful addition to what a church can do. There are times when sickness and infirmity prevent us from gathering together, not to mention a pandemic season! Livestreaming is a great blessing. But it can also be a curse. It can create a laziness about in-person participation. It is not a substitute for the real thing. And for some, who prefer their own company to the social environment of a church service, a proverb comes to mind: "Whoever isolates himself seeks his own desire; he breaks out against all sound judgment" (Prov. 18:1).

We gather "to stir up one another." The Greek word is the word from which we get the English word *paroxysm*. The King James Version translates it "provoke." It is a word that we often associate with ideas of irritation and exasperation! And while exasperation may be going too far, encouraging "one another to love and good works" (v. 24) can be unsettling when habits of self-centeredness obscure our calling.

When Paul and Barnabas disagreed over the employment of John Mark after the latter's failure in the Apostle's first missionary journey, Luke writes, "And there arose a sharp disagreement [*paroxysmos*], so that they separated from each other" (Acts 15:39). Here in Hebrews 10, the word has an intensity that joins us together instead of separating us. You need to be in the company of your brothers and sisters who love you enough to help you navigate the right course and do what God wants you to do.

It's Not All about *You*

Fourth, there is the issue of *usefulness*. The nonattendance of some that the author of Hebrews writes about reflects a fundamental misunderstanding of what the church is supposed to be. Some were neglecting corporate gathering. The word "neglect" is the word "forsaken" used by Jesus on the cross: "My God, my God, why have you forsaken me?" (Mark 15:34). Some had forsaken the church, cut off all connection with it, viewing the church as nonessential and irrelevant.

This attitude touches upon a fundamental issue that says a great deal about us and our culture. I refer to the tendency to say, "I don't get much out of church." But perhaps the more important question should be, "What are you putting into the church?" If your view of spiritual growth and godliness is almost exclusively about you and your relationship with Jesus, church might appear less than necessary. After all, you can get in touch with your inner self anywhere, especially when you are alone.

Church is not a spectator sport.[13] I sometimes quip that the Evangelical National Anthem of the United States begins, "O say can you see, what's in it for me?" Christians often complain because they perceive that the sole purpose of the church is to make them feel better about themselves. This view is wrong on so many levels, and it misses the fact that one function of the church is to enable us to serve one another. The three words that stabilize our thinking are *others,*

others, others. The Apostle Paul addresses this very issue in a letter he wrote to a dysfunctional church in the city of Corinth:

> For just as the body is one and has many members, and all the members of the body, though many, are one body, so it is with Christ. For in one Spirit we were all baptized into one body—Jews or Greeks, slaves or free—and all were made to drink of one Spirit.
>
> For the body does not consist of one member but of many. If the foot should say, "Because I am not a hand, I do not belong to the body," that would not make it any less a part of the body. And if the ear should say, "Because I am not an eye, I do not belong to the body," that would not make it any less a part of the body. If the whole body were an eye, where would be the sense of hearing? If the whole body were an ear, where would be the sense of smell? But as it is, God arranged the members in the body, each one of them, as he chose. If all were a single member, where would the body be? As it is, there are many parts, yet one body.
>
> The eye cannot say to the hand, "I have no need of you," nor again the head to the feet, "I have no need of you." On the contrary, the parts of the body that seem to be weaker are indispensable, and on those parts of the body that we think less honorable we bestow the greater honor, and our unpresentable parts are treated with greater modesty, which our more presentable parts do not require. But God has so composed the body, giving greater honor to the part that lacked it, that there may be no division in the body, but that the members may have the same care for one another. If one member suffers, all suffer together; if one member is honored, all rejoice together.
>
> Now you are the body of Christ and individually members of it. (1 Cor. 12:12–27)

Every member has a ministry to perform. Not a single member is redundant. The church needs you, and you need the church. The entire body prospers when every member is fully engaged. "We are to grow up in every way into him who is the head, into Christ, from whom the whole body, joined and held together by every joint with which it is equipped, when each part is working properly, makes the body grow so that it builds itself up in love" (Eph. 4:15–16).

Neglecting the Church

So, we have established the importance of the church in our Christian life. We are to assemble together. Practically, what does this require-ment to assemble involve? Should I be at every meeting the church has? Probably not, if the church has too many meetings—and that can and does happen. Let's put it a different way. Should I be present for worship on Sunday? Yes! We will look at this in a separate chap-ter, but for now, it is important to note that attendance on Sunday is not an optional matter—at least, it is not optional if the fourth com-mandment is still operative, and there is not a shred of evidence that the New Testament requires only nine of the Ten Commandments.

But we need to be a little more discerning as to what the author of Hebrews is suggesting: "not neglecting to meet together, as is the habit of some, but encouraging one another."

"not neglecting . . . but encouraging one another"

The contrast envisaged is not that of attending versus not attend-ing. The contrast is between neglecting the body and encouraging the body. That means that you can show up and still neglect the body. If all you do is show up, you are not ministering to the body. If you don't speak to anyone, greet a visitor, ask about someone's family, encourage a brother or sister who is passing through difficulties, or offer to pray with someone who is anxious or discouraged, then you are not ministering to the body. And your eager, joyful engagement in worship is also a ministry to others. There is safety in numbers.

The Second Coming

The author of Hebrews adds one more incentive for gathered assemblies of God's people: "all the more as you see the Day drawing near" (Heb. 10:25).

Why should gathering for worship on Sundays bring to mind the second coming? It may not be intuitive, but the reason lies in something that the writer of Hebrews has mentioned earlier in his letter. Warning of the possibility of apostasy in chapter 6, he adds that the covenant community experiences "the powers of the age to come" (Heb. 6:5). When we worship together, we join our worship with angels and archangels and the church "on the other side." Jesus sings alongside us in worship.

Think of it like this: there is another dimension where the saints triumphant are alive and reigning with Christ. Something of "the end" has broken through into the "now."

> Now these things happened to them as an example, but they were written down for our instruction, on whom the end of the ages has come. (1 Cor. 10:11; cf. Heb. 9:26)

As Christians we sit "in the heavenly places in Christ Jesus" (Eph. 2:6). The world to come has broken through into our world. And as we worship, we do so in anticipation of what is to come. Here and now, we see only dimly; but there we shall see Jesus "face to face" (1 Cor. 13:12).

Earlier in the letter, the author quotes from Psalm 22:

For he who sanctifies and those who are sanctified all have one source. That is why he is not ashamed to call them brothers, saying,

"I will tell of your name to my brothers;
in the midst of the congregation I will sing your praise."
(Heb. 2:11–12)

It is as though he is saying to us that every time we worship together, Jesus is singing along with us, as if He were standing next to us, sharing a hymnbook! Imagine how that image might radically alter the way we approach worship.

Assembling together as a church body is a reminder that this world is not our home. Jesus is coming again, and when He does, He will usher in the new heavens and new earth. But the author sounds a fearful alarm. With the dawning of "the Day" comes the reality of a day of judgment: "For if we go on sinning deliberately after receiving the knowledge of the truth, there no longer remains a sacrifice for sins, but a fearful expectation of judgment, and a fury of fire that will consume the adversaries" (Heb. 10:26–27).

Great restaurants may offer a range of culinary experiences: "A Taste of Mexico," "A Taste of Italy," or "A Taste of America." Sunday worship should advertise a similar experience: "A Taste of Heaven."

2

Keeping Sunday Special

My ten-year-old grandson told his father the other day that he wasn't sure if he knew all the Ten Commandments and that perhaps he should learn them, in case he might be breaking one of them!

Of all the Ten Commandments, one always seems to cause a problem—the fourth, on the Sabbath day. Simply put, is the New Testament Lord's Day the moral and legal equivalent of the Old Testament Sabbath? Or, perhaps oversimplifying it, are we obligated to keep the fourth commandment, or should we cut bait and say we have nine commandments, not ten?[1] Putting this another way, is there a *moral* obligation to keep one day in seven *holy*? If not, as those who argue that no such *moral* obligation exists, why retain a *seven*-day week? It is logical that one of the things advocated during the French Revolution was a *ten*-day week.[2]

Nothing like starting a chapter with some provocation!

In addition, there is another problem: the allegation that insisting on compliance to the fourth commandment is "legalistic." Once that term is thrown out, it tends to stick regardless of whether it is remotely justifiable. If we are supposed to keep the commandment, it is not legalistic to do so. And if we are, the $64,000 question is, *How?*

Not every Christian with a low view of the Lord's Day can give a theological explanation for his position. However, those who have sought some theological justification for downplaying the fourth commandment raise (at least) these two considerations:

1. While the other nine commandments are mentioned in the New Testament, the fourth is not specifically mentioned.

2. The New Testament views the fourth commandment as fulfilled in Christ. The "rest" required in the Old Testament commandment functioned solely as a *ceremonial* depiction of the "rest" of the gospel—that we are saved by faith alone in Christ alone, and "apart from works of the law" (Rom. 3:28; see Gal. 2:16). The legal requirement (like the Levitical sacrificial system) pointed to its fulfillment in Christ. Once Christ completed His mediatorial function, the requirement to obey the Sabbath commandment ceased. Some argue that this is what Paul suggests in Romans 14:5 ("One person esteems one day as better than another, while another esteems all days alike. Each one should be fully convinced in his own mind") and Colossians 2:16 ("Therefore let no one pass judgment on you in questions of food and drink, or with regard to a festival or a new moon or a Sabbath"). Clearly, *some* ceremonial aspect has been fulfilled, but is it the weekly Sabbath that is in view?

The answer to the second point is that Colossians and Romans are referencing the ceremonial *holy days* rather than the Sabbath in Levitical law.[3] Christians are under no obligation to obey the feast days of the Old Testament ceremonial calendar.

Furthermore, there is indeed an aspect of the *weekly* Sabbath "rest" that is fulfilled in Christ. Indeed, the change of day from the last day to the first day of the week can be seen as signaling this very fulfillment: in the Old Testament, the period of anticipation, there was a cycle of work followed by rest; in the New Testament, it is the other way around—rest is followed by work. This rhythm reflects the gospel age of the new covenant. This is not to suggest that the old covenant was devoid of the gospel. Rather, it simply reflects what Paul suggests when he likens the old covenant administration to a "ministry of death" and "condemnation," in contrast to the new covenant, which is depicted as a "ministry of the Spirit" and of "glory" and of "righteousness" (2 Cor. 3:7–11). It is a case of a relative contrast stated in absolute terms, as John does when he writes, "For the law was given through Moses; grace and truth came through Jesus Christ" (John 1:17). John does not intend to suggest that there was no grace and truth under Mosaic rule any more than he intended his readers to understand that the new covenant era has no rules for Christians to obey.

Remember the Sabbath Day

When the Ten Commandments are introduced in Exodus 20 (and repeated on the verge of entry to the promised land in Deuteronomy 5), the fourth commandment begins with the verb "Remember": "Remember the Sabbath day, to keep it holy" (Ex. 20:8). This is not the first time that a commandment to observe one day as different from the rest has been made. The commandment was given in the creation story in Genesis 1:1–2:3. From the very beginning of time, the seventh day had been singled out as special because it reflects something about the way God created the universe. He brought it into being in *six* days and on the *seventh* day, "he rested . . . from all his work that he had done" (Gen. 2:2). That principle of obedience is now underscored at Sinai.

The Sabbath was *first of all* a reflection of the pattern and rhythm of creation: work and rest. And its abrogation would imply that there is no longer any rhythm to our life. Weekly rhythms are important.

God blessed one day in seven so that His people might "keep it holy" (separate, different, special). And what is remarkable is that the early Christians began almost immediately to change the rhythm but *not* to abandon the principle—to begin each week with a rest day and follow it with days of work. As Christians, we need to recapture this outlook by abandoning the secular rhythm of *the weekend*.

There is no discussion about the Lord's Day in the early church. There is no specific reiteration of the requirement in the early church; there is only the record that it happened. Christians began to keep one day special because the pattern of redemptive life had always suggested a change in rhythm. And the day of Christ's resurrection from the grave seemed the obvious and natural day to set apart. In the words of B.B. Warfield, "Christ took the Sabbath into the grave with him and brought the Lord's Day out of the grave with him on the resurrection morn."[4] Something of the old covenant had been fulfilled; something of the new needed a new way of demonstrating how the fourth commandment now operates. The Old Testament "Sabbath" and the New Testament "Lord's Day" are, therefore, in principle, one and the same.

Caveats

Having established the requirement to observe the keeping of the Lord's Day as special in the rhythm of the Christian life, we now need to explore the manner in which this is to be done.

First, we should be careful about dismissing the fourth commandment by the use of the word *legalism*.

Christians sometimes use the word *legalism* as a synonym for "this is inconvenient." Knowing that compliance with the fourth commandment may cause one to alter lifestyle habits or behavior, our conscience finds temporary relief under the shade of the term *legalism*. When this is done, Christians are not using the term in its strict and accurate sense, which is requiring obedience for the sake of gaining favor with God or requiring obedience to man-made laws.[5] In both of these instances, *legalism* is the correct word. However, it is *not* legalistic to require compliance with something God requires of us.

Second, Sunday is a day for public worship. Sunday, the Lord's Day, is holy in a way that other days are not. It is a day set apart for the public gathering of God's people. As we saw in the previous chapter, we are urged in Hebrews not to neglect public gathering on the Lord's Day (Heb. 10:25).

Sundays provide opportunities for worship and the fulfillment of Jesus' promise in Matthew 18:20: "For where two or three are gathered in my name, there am I among them." There is nothing quite like the experience of the presence of Christ in our gathered worship. The Lord's Day also provides opportunities for Sunday schools where the Bible is studied and a venue to enjoy some more informal fellowship with brothers and sisters in Christ.

Whenever we gather as a church on the Lord's Day, we are participating in the greatest mystery and most wonderful experience that any individual or group of redeemed human beings could ever know—the experience of the unity of the body and bride of Christ with Him who was slain and rose again for sins.

Third, we need to be intentional about keeping Sunday *special*. I have little interest in answering questions of casuistry: "Can I do *x* or *y* on Sunday?" Questions like this invariably start at the wrong end. It is like the child who is told he cannot leave a certain place. Inevitably, the child will walk up to the imaginary line you have drawn and then begin to inch across to see if you will respond. If we are correct in suggesting that in principle the Old Testament Sabbath is the same as the New Testament Lord's Day, how are we meant to ensure that the day (according to the fourth commandment) is kept "holy"?

Many Christians have to work on Sundays (or at least a part of it). There are vocations that are essential for the stability and health of society. Early Jewish Christians worked on the Lord's Day and had to make concessions for worship early on Sunday mornings.

It has been relatively easy for me, since I'm a minister of the gospel, to keep Sunday *special*. I have no choice in what I do on Sunday. And I have also been in churches the entirety of my Christian life where there were at least two services, morning and evening, to attend. I did not have the luxury of asking, What am I going to *do* on this day?

Every family has to make decisions about what keeping the Lord's Day holy means for them. Getting into situations that mean I consistently miss worship for weeks and months because I want my children to be involved in competitive sports on Sunday seems misguided. What will my children think of church if their childhood involved so little of it?

At this point, it is all too easy to become judgmental about others. For those who engage in manual labor all week, Sunday afternoon may be the one day in the week where you take a long nap. For those who sit at a desk all week, perhaps Sunday afternoon is a day you take a long walk. The last thing we should be doing is judging one another.

Should we insist that every Christian attend every service the church advertises? Should Christians be obligated to attend morning and (if there is one) evening worship? For my part, I have no regrets that for almost half a century the rhythm of morning and evening worship has consistently been present in my life. Historically, the church introduced it to reflect the rhythm of morning and evening worship in the temple. And, while great benefit can be obtained by observing this practice (where it is available), there is no biblical mandate for it. I think it depends on what you replace Sunday evening worship with and whether that fulfills the need to make the Lord's Day *special*.

Fifth, be intentional about receiving the maximum amount from the worship service. Our forefathers did this by preparing on Saturday night. Meals were semi-prepared to ensure maximum involvement in the Lord's Day and enjoyment of the physical rest that it affords. None of this need be viewed as "legalistic" if the profit more than makes up for the inconvenience. The Sabbath, the Lord's Day, was given *for us*—to help us grow in grace and to prevent work from becoming our master and us its slave. John Stott makes the same point: "The climax of Genesis 1 is not the creation of human beings as workers but the institution of the Sabbath for human beings as worshippers. The end point is not our toil (subduing the earth) but the laying aside of our toil on the Sabbath day. For the Sabbath puts the importance of work into perspective. It protects us from a total absorption in our work as if it were to be the be-all and end-all of our existence. It is not."[6]

Loving the Lord's Day

Alexander Whyte once wrote in a commentary on the Westminster Shorter Catechism: "There is perhaps no surer sign of a falling Christian than a growing neglect of Sabbath day ordinances, and an indolent and profane abuse of its sacred and priceless hours. There is no bulwark that parents can build up around their children's religion and morality like a well-kept Sabbath day; and there is no surer sign that a young man is declining from faith and personal religion than when he begins to find his own pleasure and do his own way on the Lord's holy day."[7]

As we have seen, the Sabbath was inaugurated not at Sinai but in the paradise of Eden (Gen. 2:2–3). At that moment, the Sabbath could not have had *any* ceremonial or typical significance of a redemptive nature. It was a gift to humanity to ensure that the work given them to do would also be accompanied by a weekly day of rest. A day free from the burden of work! A day to reflect on and enjoy who God is and what He has promised for His children. A day to focus on *worship*!

Few things remain special unless we approach them with some degree of purposefulness. We make an effort to make vacations, birthdays, and anniversaries special. We should make an effort to ensure that we derive the maximum profit from the Lord's Day. After all, the Puritans referred to the Lord's Day as "the market day for the soul." In addition to gathered worship, we could catch up on Bible reading, pray, visit with family, visit a shut-in, take a nap, or go for a walk.

We can also make sure that children do not find Sundays tedious.

Too often, we have not made Sundays a delight for them. We should try to teach them about how special the day is. And we should avoid making Sundays a "thou shalt *not*" day! In our family, we often had chocolate on Sunday afternoons.

Christian Holiness

By setting the requirement to observe a weekly pattern of rest followed by work, a pattern that, in principle, extends the application of the fourth commandment into the new covenant era, God placed the Sabbath as a fundamental aspect of Christian holiness. One important aspect of the law is to provide for us the contours of Christian holiness. Our personal sanctification—that is to say, our Christlikeness, for that is what sanctification basically demonstrates (Rom. 8:29)—is measured precisely by the obedience we render to the fourth commandment.

The Reformation outlined three "uses" of the law. The first use was to highlight God's righteousness and our sinfulness: "If it had not been for the law, I would not have known sin" (Rom. 7:7). The second use of the law is its civic function, providing the shape of civic duty and threatening punishment for those who transgress (Rom. 13:3–4). The third use of the law is to provide guidelines for Christians of patterns of behavior that please God. Christians are free from the law as a means of salvation (Rom. 6:14; 7:4, 6; 1 Cor. 9:20; Gal. 2:15–19; 3:25), but they are "under the law of Christ" as a rule of life (1 Cor. 9:21; see Gal. 6:2).

When I became a Christian (during my first semester at university), the Lord's Day became a cherished pattern of my life. I had not grown up in a Christian home and I had rarely attended a church. However, conversion changed all that, and for the last fifty years the rhythm of morning and evening worship on the Lord's Day has been normative. Hardly ever have I found the sanctification of the first day of the week a burden. On the contrary, it has proved a means of grace and growth. I made a decision from the very beginning that I would not study on the Lord's Day, not even if I had an examination on Monday morning! I have, more or less, kept this pattern for the last fifty years, and I have no regrets. On the contrary, the sheer difference of the Lord's Day, even as a preacher who technically "works" on Sunday, provides both structure and stability to my Christian life. And on the few Sundays when emergencies took place—the "ox in the ditch" moments (Luke 14:5)—the lack of the Sunday rhythm was made worse by the absence of the benefits that being with God's people in worship provide. The fact that I felt I had genuinely "missed" worship as well as the rest of the Lord's Day was in some sense reassuring.

Since the rest of the Lord's Day finds its ultimate fulfillment in the gospel, the Lord's Day proves to be a little taste of heaven.

3

The Regulative Principle

Are there any guidelines for formal gathered worship services? The question appears loaded, and it is. Too often, we approach worship as we might approach a restaurant menu: we choose what we want to eat according to some largely undefined subjective desire. Some prefer a more contemporary and relaxed worship service. Others prefer a heavily liturgical and classical (traditional) service. One prefers a guitar, and another prefers an organ. Welcome to the worship wars!

We cannot possibly solve all the issues raised by worship style in this brief chapter, but we can raise an important question that helps address the issue in principle: Is formal worship merely a matter of taste and preference? Putting it another way, are there any *biblical* principles that may guide us to an answer? The answer is *yes*! It is what the Reformation and post-Reformation church called the *regulative principle*.

The key word in the question above is *biblical*. Too often we approach the issue of worship style subjectively. We find ourselves more comfortable with one style than another and do not stop to ask if there are any biblical guiding principles to help us make a more informed decision.

What is the regulative principle? Put simply, the regulative principle of worship states that the corporate worship of God is to be founded on specific directives of Scripture. Put another way, it states that nothing ought to be introduced into gathered worship unless there is a specific warrant of Scripture.

Let us be clear: we worship God in "all of life"—when fishing, playing golf, eating breakfast, or driving a car. Paul makes this very clear: "I appeal to you therefore, brothers, by the mercies of God, to present your bodies as a living sacrifice, holy and acceptable to God, which is your spiritual worship. Do not be conformed to this world, but be transformed by the renewal of your mind, that by testing you may discern what is the will of God, what is good and acceptable and perfect" (Rom. 12:1–2).

Because of this, some have argued that there is no special set of rules for gathered worship. There's just worship! But this ignores some very important issues. True, there is a regulative principle (a set of general rules) for what we might call "all of life" worship. Everything we do must have in view the glory of God. "So, whether you eat or drink, or whatever you do, do all to the glory of God" (1 Cor. 10:31). We might call this a *general* regulative principle. But is there a more specific application of this principle for gathered worship? The Reformers (John Calvin especially) and the Puritans answered *yes*. God is especially concerned as to the question of *how* we worship in public gatherings.

Typical by way of formulation are the words of Calvin: "God disapproves of all modes of worship not expressly sanctioned by his Word,"[1] and the Second London Baptist Confession of 1689: "The acceptable way of worshiping the true God, is instituted by himself, and so limited by his own revealed will, that he may not be worshiped according to the imagination and devices of men, nor the suggestions of Satan, under any visible representations, or any other way not pre-scribed in the Holy Scriptures."[2]

The Westminster Assembly

When the Westminster Assembly gathered, its primary directive was to answer this very question. It soon began to address other issues, but it was the issue of worship that dominated its initial agenda. It would later publish a Directory for the Public Worship of God. The term *directory* is itself important; it is not a Book of Common Prayer as the Anglicans had. They were very clear that the directory func-tioned in a very different way.

The very first chapter of the Westminster Confession of Faith is about Scripture. It was a way of saying that before we can say any-thing about God or humanity or sin or the church, or *worship*, we need some *basis of authority*. And that sole authority is the Word of God. All of Scripture is a product of God's outbreathing (2 Tim. 3:16–17). Men spoke as they were driven along by the Holy Spirit (2 Peter 1:21). For the Westminster tradition, then, we begin with Scripture.

It is in this opening chapter on Scripture as the foundation of all knowledge that the regulative principle appears:

The whole counsel of God concerning all things necessary for his own glory, man's salvation, faith and life, is either expressly set down in Scripture, or by good and necessary consequence may be deduced from Scripture: unto which nothing at any time is to be added, whether by new revelations of the Spirit, or traditions of men. Nevertheless, we acknowledge the inward illumination of the Spirit of God to be necessary for the saving understanding of such things as are revealed in the Word: and that there are some circumstances concerning the worship of God, and government of the Church, common to human actions and societies, which are to be ordered by the light of nature, and Christian prudence, according to the general rules of the Word, which are always to be observed. (WCF 1.6)

The point being made is that Scripture lays down certain principles about two particular issues (there are others): the form of church government and public worship. The same principle appears again in the chapter on worship:

The light of nature shows that there is a God, who has lordship and sovereignty over all, is good, and does good unto all, and is therefore to be feared, loved, praised, called upon, trusted in, and served, with all the heart, and with all the soul, and with all the might. But the acceptable way of worshipping the true God is instituted by Himself, and so limited by His own revealed will, that He may not be worshipped according to the imaginations and devices of men, or the suggestions of Satan, under any visible representation, or any other way not prescribed in the holy Scripture. (WCF 21.1)

The point is that Scripture (that is, God Himself, since Scripture is God's Word) *prescribes* how we worship God. The word *prescribe* carries the idea of authority. When you go to the drugstore and you need some medicine that isn't an "over the counter" drug, you need a prescription—it used to be a piece of paper signed by the doctor (these days it is usually done electronically).

And why did the Westminster divines (the theologians who gathered at the Westminster Assembly) think this was so important? The answer to that lies in the previous chapter of the confession, which is arguably the most important chapter in the confession and one that is set in a very special context in the seventeenth century—the chapter on liberty of conscience. It contains this vitally important statement: "God alone is Lord of the conscience and has left it free from the doctrines and commandments of men, which are, in anything, contrary to His Word; or beside it, if matters of faith, or worship" (WCF 20:2).

To *insist* on a certain action in worship that Scripture does not expressly command is to violate freedom of conscience. That was a vital issue in the seventeenth century. For the founding fathers of the United States of America, for example, this was a vital issue. Freedom of conscience was the only guarantee of religious liberty.

The Westminster Assembly was established in the wake of attempts on the part of the king (and the Church of England) to impose a manner of worship upon Scotland. And some of the Scots weren't having any of it. There is the compelling story of Jenny Geddes, for example. In 1637, Charles I attempted to impose an English-style prayer book upon the nation of Scotland. The legend goes that "when Dean James Hannay began to read from it, . . . a local woman named Jenny Geddes hurled at his head the folding stool on which she had been seated, shouting, 'Dinna say Mass in my lug!' ('Don't say Mass in my ear!')."[3]

To impose rituals and ceremonies with religious significance that do not have express scriptural support is to violate conscience.

Scriptural Warrant for the Regulative Principle[4]

Where does the Bible teach the regulative principle? In more places than is commonly imagined, including the constant stipulation of the book of Exodus with respect to the building of the tabernacle that everything be done "after the pattern ... shown you" (Ex. 25:40). Add to this the judgment pronounced on Cain's offering, which suggests that his offering (or his heart) was deficient according to God's requirement (Gen. 4:3–8); the first and second commandments, which show God's particular care with regard to worship (Ex. 20:2–6); the incident of the golden calf, which teaches that worship cannot be offered merely in accord with our own values and tastes; the story of Nadab and Abihu and the offering of "strange fire" (Lev. 10, KJV); God's rejection of Saul's non-prescribed worship—God said, "To obey is better than sacrifice" (1 Sam. 15:22); and Jesus' rejection of Pharisaical worship according to the "tradition of the elders" (Matt. 15:1–14). All these indicate a rejection of worship offered according to values and directions other than those specified in Scripture.

Of particular significance are Paul's responses to errant public worship at Colossae and Corinth. At one point, Paul characterizes the public worship in Colossae as *ethelothrēskia* (Col. 2:23), variously translated as "will worship" (KJV) or "self-made religion" (ESV). The Colossians had introduced elements that were clearly unacceptable (even if they were claiming an angelic source for their actions—one possible interpretation of Col. 2:18, the "worship of angels").

Perhaps it is in the Corinthian use (abuse) of tongues and prophecy that we find the clearest indication of the Apostle's willingness to "regulate" corporate worship. He regulates both the number and order of the use of spiritual gifts in a way that does not apply to "all of life": no tongue is to be employed without an interpreter (1 Cor. 14:27–28), and only two or three prophets may speak, in turn (vv. 29–32). At the very least, Paul's instruction to the Corinthians underlines that corporate worship is to be regulated and in a manner that applies differently from that which is true for all of life.

The result? Particular elements of worship are highlighted:

- Reading the Bible (1 Tim. 4:13)
- Preaching the Bible (2 Tim. 4:2)
- Singing the Bible (Eph. 5:19; Col. 3:16)—the Psalms as well as Scripture songs that reflect the development of redemptive history in the birth, life, death, resurrection, and ascension of Jesus
- Praying the Bible—the Father's house is "a house of prayer" (Matt. 21:13)
- Seeing the Bible in the two sacraments of the church—baptism and the Lord's Supper, something Augustine referred to as "visible words"[5] (Matt. 28:19; Acts 2:38–39; 1 Cor. 11:23–26; Col. 2:11–12). In addition, occasional elements such as oaths, vows, solemn fasts, and thanksgivings have also been recognized and highlighted (see WCF 21:5).

And that's it!

It is important to realize that the regulative principle as applied to public worship frees the church from acts of impropriety and idiocy—we are not free, for example, to advertise that performing clowns will mime the Bible lesson at next week's Sunday service.

The regulative principle is just that—a *principle*. It doesn't answer every single question one may throw at it. And because of that, it does not commit the church to a "cookie-cutter," liturgical sameness. Within an adherence to the principle there is considerable room for variation—in matters that Scripture has not specifically addressed (*adiaphora*). Thus, the regulative principle as such may not be invoked to determine whether contemporary or traditional songs are employed, whether three verses or three chapters of Scripture are read, whether one long prayer or several short prayers are made, or whether a single cup or individual cups with real wine or grape juice are used at the Lord's Supper. To all these issues, the principle "all things should be done decently and in order" (1 Cor. 14:40) must be applied.

Some employ the regulative principle to construct a worship service that is more liturgically "heavy" than others. Scottish and Irish Presbyterianism, for example, followed the liturgical pattern of the Puritans rather than the Reformation and therefore are liturgically "light."

However, if someone were to suggest that dancing or drama is a valid aspect of public worship, the question must be asked, Where is the biblical justification for it? To suggest that a preacher moving about in the pulpit or employing "dramatic" voices is "drama" in the sense above is to trivialize the debate. The fact that both may be (to employ the colloquialism) "neat" is debatable and beside the point; there is no shred of biblical evidence, let alone mandate, for either. So it is superfluous to argue from the poetry of the Psalms or the example of David dancing before the ark (in a state of undress!) unless we are willing to abandon all the received rules of biblical interpretation. It is a salutary fact that no office of "choreographer" or "producer/

director" existed in the temple. The fact that both dance and drama are valid Christian pursuits is also beside the point.

Without the regulative principle, we are at the mercy of "worship leaders" and bullying pastors who charge noncompliant worshipers with displeasing God unless they participate according to a certain pattern and manner. To obey when it is a matter of God's express prescription is true liberty; anything else is bondage and legalism.

In closing this chapter, I cite the appropriate words of Ligon Duncan as he describes the regulative principle:

> Since our worship is for God, our first question is not, "What do we want to do?" or even "What would others like to do?" but "What does God want us to do?" For direction we look to the Bible where God directs by command or approved example how to worship Him. In the Bible we find God accepting these acts of worship: Singing, praying, reading the Bible, preaching, celebrating sacraments, giving offerings, confessing the faith, and making holy vows.
>
> We want to assure that our corporate worship is Bible-filled and Bible-directed, that the substance and structure are biblical, that the content and order are biblical. To put it slightly differently, we want to worship "by the book" in two ways: so that both the marrow and means of worship are according to Scripture. We want the form and substance of corporate worship to be suffused with Scripture and scriptural theology.[6]

4

Liturgy-Lite

*L*iturgy is derived from the Greek word *leitourgia* and translated in the ESV as either "ministry" or "service." We often use the word *service* for a time of public worship. In the previous chapter, we spoke of the regulative principle and concluded that when we gather for public worship, we are to do what God has prescribed, and *only* what God has prescribed. In brief compass, that means that we read the Bible, pray the Bible, sing the Bible, preach the Bible, and (in the sacraments) see the Bible.

But how are these elements of worship to be done? In what order should they appear? What weight should be given to each component? In the Presbyterian tradition, the answer to these questions was given in the form of a document known as the Directory for the Public Worship of God, known in Scotland as the Westminster Directory and approved by the Scottish Parliament in 1645.

The directory is not what one might expect, in that it does not provide any set liturgy. Rather, it outlines instructions to ministers on a wide range of pastoral practice, including a lengthy section on visiting the sick and a detailed section on preaching. Part of the reason it did not provide a set liturgy (as the Book of Common Prayer does, for example) was the authors' very adherence to the regulative principle and the requirement for biblical prescription. The Bible, after all, does not provide a *specific* liturgy.

The Bible does not give us "an order of worship," and imposing one would violate the regulative principle. That means that Presbyterians have viewed the shape of the liturgy in different ways. In Scottish and Irish Presbyterian churches, it is uncommon to have a printed liturgy, for example, and the service therefore contains few if any "responses" by the congregation. In the United States, the liturgy is almost always printed and therefore appears to be more liturgical. The regulative principle provides freedom to put the parts of the liturgy together in different ways and does not force a fixed liturgy upon all churches.

It is interesting to note what Luke tells us about the early church after Pentecost. Summarizing, Luke tells us that "they devoted themselves to the apostles' teaching and the fellowship, to the breaking of bread and the prayers" (Acts 2:42). The early church met in people's homes ("house churches"), and perhaps the reference to "breaking of bread" alludes to a fellowship meal rather than the Lord's Supper. It is, however, the reference to *"the* prayers" and the use of the definite article that is of interest. It suggests that they were repeating "set prayers" of some kind. Certainly, the synagogue had a fixed liturgy. It looked like this:

- Open with prayer (the *Shema* of Deut. 6:4–5)
- Two introductory benedictions
- Reading of the Ten Commandments and sections of the Pentateuch

- Eighteen prayers and benedictions (called the *berachoth*)
- A lesson/reading from the Law and a lesson from the Prophets
- Homily
- Benediction[1]

No doubt these were maintained and supplemented as Christians began to pray in the name of Jesus and began to reference what Jesus' death and resurrection meant by way of atonement and forgiveness.

At the time of the European Reformation, considerable attention was given to the issue of public worship. Sinclair Ferguson has written:

> They [the Reformers] well understood that the rediscovery of the gospel and the reformation of worship were two sides of the same coin, because sung praise, confessions of sin and confessions of Faith, prayer, and the reading and preaching of Scripture are but various aspects of the one ministry of the Word. For that reason, the Reformers regarded the liturgies that framed the Church's worship as being an important aspect of the application of Scripture. An order of service could not therefore be simply thrown together casually. It might belong to the *adiaphora*;[2] but "things indifferent" are never treated with indifference to the general teaching of Scripture (as the Westminster Divines would later make clear).[3]

Medieval worship, in the form of the Latin Mass, was well-nigh incomprehensible to the listener (who understood little or no Latin).

Consequently, worship became a spectacle—something visual and dramatic. It was more about music and ceremony that someone else performed. The massive change brought by the Reformation was that services were conducted in the mother tongue, and congregational participation (in singing, for example) was encouraged.

God-Centered Worship

What characteristics of worship should the liturgy enhance?

First, the liturgy should convey the importance of *God-centered worship*. Jesus told the woman of Samaria something very important about worship. At one level, we should ask, Why is He talking to her at all about worship? The answer is simple. He came to save sinners in order that they, in turn, would worship God as they have never done before. "The hour is coming," Jesus told her, "and is now here, when the true worshipers will worship the Father in spirit and truth, for the Father is seeking such people to worship him. God is spirit, and those who worship him must worship in spirit and truth" (John 4:23–24).

The use of a biblically informed liturgy frees us from the tyranny of "worship leaders" who often interject their own thoughts and opinions. Inevitably, the service can take on something of the personality of the worship leader. "I'm feeling down today, so we are going to sing a rather sad song," or "I'm having a wonderful day, and you all need to be rejoicing with me." This kind of man-centered worship is nothing short of idolatry. God is seeking worshipers. The one to whom we must be sensitive is not the worshiper; it is God!

By way of contrast, think of those God-centered moments of heavenly worship described in Isaiah and Revelation where day and night seraphim fly before the face of God singing, "Holy, holy, holy is the LORD of hosts; the whole earth is full of his glory!" (Isa. 6:3);

angelic creatures fly before Him calling to one another, "Holy, holy, holy, is the Lord God Almighty, who was and is and is to come!" (Rev. 4:8); the twenty-four angelic elders fall down before Him casting down their crowns, saying, "Worthy are you, our Lord and God, to receive glory and honor and power, for you created all things, and by your will they existed and were created" (Rev. 4:11).

It is this aspect of a sense of God's presence in holiness and glory that is at the heart of Paul's *liturgical* concern in the Corinthian church, troubled as it was with the misuse of the Apostolic sign-gifts of tongues and prophecy: "If . . . an unbeliever or outsider enters, he is convicted . . . he is called to account . . . the secrets of his heart are disclosed, and so, falling on his face, he will worship God and declare that God is really among you" (1 Cor. 14:24–25). The flow of worship directed by the liturgy ought to have that effect—to underline that God is among us and we are to worship *Him*. Liturgy is not, therefore, simply a matter of *what works* or what pleases this or that subgroup or even the majority; it is about ordering what Scripture prescribes in a manner that will give God most glory.

Second, the liturgy must be *dialogical*. The liturgy is a holy dialogue between God and His people. It is not simply a one-way conversation. God speaks (through His Word), and we respond in prayer, in confession of sin, and in confession of faith. At the beginning of the service, there is a call to worship. A typical example would be the opening words of Psalm 95:

> Oh come, let us sing to the LORD;
>> let us make a joyful noise to the rock of our salvation!
> Let us come into his presence with thanksgiving;
>> let us make a joyful noise to him with songs of praise!

For the LORD is a great God,
> and a great King above all gods.
In his hand are the depths of the earth;
> the heights of the mountains are his also.
The sea is his, for he made it,
> and his hands formed the dry land.

Oh come, let us worship and bow down;
> let us kneel before the LORD, our Maker! (vv. 1–6)

After the call to worship, we sing God's praise and then we pray the prayer of invocation. The word *invocation* comes from the Latin *invocare*, meaning "to call upon." It is typically brief in compass and sharp in focus. In it, we call on God to come down to us, to receive our worship, to bless us as a congregation. And so, the dialogue continues through the service until the final word from God—the benediction.

Listening to God in Scripture and responding in prayer and praise and confession means we need to be intentional about worship. It is not a time to drift off and recall the ten things we need to do before the day is through. We need to give all our attention to the worship of God. That means we must think and feel appropriately. A bulletin is helpful in ensuring some intentionality and seriousness.

Third, the liturgy should be essentially *simple*. Think, by way of contrast, of Old Testament worship, with its sacrifices, rituals, purification ceremonies, and complex calendar. In order for the Levitical priesthood to properly carry out their tasks in the temple, they first had to comply with an intricate set of rituals that covers the first sixteen chapters of Leviticus. New Testament worship, on the other hand, is simple. There are no dress codes, though we legalistically impose them on ourselves, binding ourselves to the elemental principles of the world much like the Colossians were accused of doing (see Col. 2:14–23). D.G. Hart writes: "Worship in the age of the Holy Spirit is not flashy or visibly powerful but instead so simple that it appears to be inconsequential. Yet the Spirit transforms these simple means (Word, prayer, and sacraments) . . . into powerful weapons of demonstrating God's glory and might, both through the conversion of sinners and through the praise and adoration of his people."[4]

Fourth, the liturgy is a way of using Scripture's principle that worship ought to be conducted in a manner that can be summarized as "decently and in order" (1 Cor. 14:40). The last thing we need on a Sunday morning is to be surprised by the innovative whims of the person leading worship. These days, the "worship leader" is typically a musician, young and highly talented in music, but often a complete novice theologically and experientially. Typically, he or she has no theological training. This has largely come about for a variety of reasons: a tendency to make music (and again, typically, sung and played by talented musicians) the central part of the "worship time" (the phrase itself calls into question what we are doing when this section is over); the understandable desire on the part of preachers to opt out of the "worship wars" by handing that over to someone else. "Thoughtless" worship is not confined to contemporary styles. Many traditional worship services show little or no thought in what is sung or what is prayed.

Fifth, the liturgy should aid in conveying *reverence and awe*. The author of Hebrews exhorts, "Let us offer to God acceptable worship, with reverence and awe" (Heb. 12:28). The reason for reverence and awe is made alarmingly clear: "for our God is a consuming fire" (v.

29). Worship is a serious engagement. It can never be done lightly or flippantly. In the book *Give Praise to God*, Don Whitney writes:

> To worship in reverence means that I humbly recognize my unworthiness before God apart from the goodness of Jesus that he has graciously credited to me. Reverence for God makes me serious minded in . . . worship. This does not mean that I'm grim or joyless; quite the contrary, but it does mean I'm not frivolous. I'm not meeting with a comedian or a clown. Since I am a child of the heavenly father, I can be at home in his loving, accepting presence. But I never forget that I am meeting with God—my maker, my judge, my king.[5]

This coming Sunday, pay attention to the order of the service and to each individual element of it. It will transform the experience of worship.

5

Scripture, Scripture, and *More* Scripture

Until I come, devote yourself to the public reading of Scripture, to exhortation, to teaching. Do not neglect the gift you have, which was given you by prophecy when the council of elders laid their hands on you. Practice these things, immerse yourself in them, so that all may see your progress. Keep a close watch on yourself and on the teaching. Persist in this, for by so doing you will save both yourself and your hearers. (1 Tim. 4:13–16)

Paul is writing to his young "son" in the faith, Timothy. The background is that Paul has been released from his first Roman imprisonment and has begun a fourth missionary journey, taking young Timothy with him and visiting some of the churches, including the church in Ephesus. After a brief stay, Paul moved on, leaving Timothy to take care of the Ephesian church. The church had some significant problems. False teachers had begun to make themselves known, spreading all kinds of heresies (1 Tim. 1:3–7; 4:1–3; 6:3–5).

In 1 Timothy 2, Paul speaks about a particularly sensitive

issue relating to certain women who were behaving ostentatiously. Imagine a young minister having to deal with that problem (vv. 9–15)! Worse, Timothy would find himself out on a limb with his fellow office bearers, some of whom had no business being chosen, and Timothy is instructed to establish the qualifications for office. Behind the need for such qualifications lies the suggestion that some of the leaders were frequently drunk and their family lives in disarray. And, what must have been terrible for Timothy to hear, he was to rebuke some of the elders publicly for failing to stop whatever it is they were doing (see 3:1–13; 5:17–22).

Then there was the chatter about how young Timothy was—and the implication that he was therefore not seasoned enough for the task (4:12). And factions existed—widows were neglected (5:3–16), and rich folk were "haughty" (6:17; see 6:7–11).

And to add to Timothy's problems, the church had not called him. He had been "placed" there by Paul, who had promptly left him and gone elsewhere. When Paul reached Macedonia, it occurred to him that his young protégé needed some instruction on how to pastor a troubled church.

And one of the things Timothy must do, and do well, is preach. Preaching is the nerve center of the church.

The Command to Preach

Paul writes to Timothy: "Until I come, devote yourself to the public reading of Scripture, to exhortation, to teaching" (1 Tim. 4:13). Three important matters emerge from the main verb in this sentence.

First, the verb "devote" is in the *present* tense. This is not something that Timothy can shelve for some future day when he has more time on his hands. Preaching and teaching are to be his current, urgent obsession. He cannot afford to neglect it. It is the first thing on his agenda. He is a preacher first and foremost.

Second, the verb is a present *imperative*. In other words, it is a command that must be executed immediately. And it isn't just an imperative; it is an *Apostolic* imperative. It comes from Timothy's mentor, who has been commissioned by none other than the risen Lord! This is not wise advice from a seasoned preacher. It is much more than that. What Paul is telling him might as well have come from God Himself.

Third, this is the *fourth* time Paul has used this verb in this letter. Earlier, Paul describes some who "devote themselves to myths" (1:4); he later refers to those who are "devoting themselves to deceitful spirits and teachings of demons" (4:1). Timothy must be committed to the truth as much as some are devoted to lies. Alarmingly, it is also the same word employed when Paul lists the qualifications of a deacon, one of which is that the individual must not be "addicted to much wine" (3:8). Preaching is to be something akin to an addiction. Gardiner Spring, a nineteenth-century pastor in New York, wrote, "The great object of every minister of the Gospel ought to be to give the services of the pulpit the pre-eminence over every other department of ministerial labor."[1]

Timothy is to *devote* himself to one principal task—teaching and preaching. The letter assumes that he is going to be a pastor, engaged in administrative matters, attending meetings with deacons and elders, overseeing the pastoral care of the congregation. But all that must take second place to preaching. In his second letter to Timothy, Paul will insist upon it again: "Preach the word" (2 Tim. 4:2).

This is why the sermon is the central feature of every worship service. It is the reason why we devote a substantial part of each service to preaching. And when other matters press for time, we have to be equally urgent to push back and ensure that adequate time is given this task.

Incarnational Communication from God

What is preaching? It is a monological discourse in which a portion of Scripture is explained and its demands powerfully enforced upon the will and heart. J.I. Packer defines preaching "as incarnational communication from God, prophetic, persuasive and powerful."[2]

In unpacking this definition, we find that preaching is first of all prophetic in the sense that when done properly, preachers act as God's mouthpiece (incarnational). Second, preaching is persuasive in the sense Paul meant when he wrote to the Corinthians saying, "We persuade others" (2 Cor. 5:11). A sermon must seek to get its listeners to engage with the text's demands and imperatives. In this sense, a sermon is more than a "talk" or a "lecture." Third, preaching should be powerful in the sense that Paul meant when he wrote "my speech and my message were not in plausible words of wisdom, but in demonstration of the Spirit and of power" (1 Cor. 2:4).

Today, many churches have almost abandoned preaching. Instead of proclaiming the Word of God by careful analysis of the Scriptures, today's preachers have succumbed to postmodernity's loss of confidence in objective truth. Al Mohler writes:

> The last few decades have been a period of wanton experimenta-
> tion in many pulpits. One of the most troubling developments is
> the decline and eclipse of expository preaching. Numerous influ-
> ential voices within evangelicalism are suggesting that the age of
> the expository sermon is now past. In its place, some contemporary

preachers now substitute messages intentionally designed to reach secular or superficial congregations—messages that avoid preaching a biblical text and thus avoid potentially embarrassing confrontation with biblical truth.[3]

Mohler cites the important observation of John A. Broadus (a founding faculty member of the Southern Baptist Theological Seminary and whose volume on preaching remains a standard to this day): "Preaching is characteristic of Christianity. No other religion has made the regular and frequent assembling of groups of people, to hear religious instruction and exhortation, an integral part of divine worship."[4]

Far too many of today's sermons reveal a loss of confidence in the power of Scripture and, sadly, embarrassment by some of its contents. One of the reasons for textual, rather than the *lectio continua* (preaching through books of the Bible, verse by verse), preaching is that sections of Scripture that offend the modern outlook can be avoided. Worse still, sermons are emptied of biblical content. They become comfortable messages aimed at pleasing and encouraging the congregation. Some sermons have little or nothing to do with the announced text. Things are said that bear no relation to what the text might be saying. Felt needs and therapeutic solutions become the agenda. But sinners do not know what their real needs are! They are unaware that the fundamental need of every individual is to know that they are sinners—by nature estranged from God and unable to do anything to rescue themselves from this malady.

As Mohler puts it: "In the end, the Christian preacher simply must confront the congregation with the Word of God. That confrontation will be at times awkward, challenging, and difficult. After all, this is the Word that pierces us like a sword. The evangelical preacher must set his aim at letting the sword loose, neither hiding it nor dulling its edge."[5]

The Pattern of Preaching

In addition to the command, Paul also explains the pattern of preaching. It consists of three parts: the public reading of Scripture, exhortation, and teaching.

The public reading of Scripture (the Greek simply says "the reading") is a carryover from the practice of the synagogue and is powerfully seen in the revival at the Water Gate in Ezra's time (Neh. 8:1–8; Luke 4:16–17; 2 Cor. 3:14).[6] The early church added to the reading of Old Testament passages the reading of Gospels and the letters of Paul, Peter, and John (cf. Col. 4:16; 1 Thess. 5:27). There is a blessing that attends the faithful reading of Scripture: "Blessed is the one who reads aloud the words of this prophecy, and blessed are those who hear, and who keep what is written in it" (Rev. 1:3).

At a time when Christians did not possess personal copies of the Scriptures, public reading was the *only* occasion when the contents of Scripture could be heard. Even so, in an age when we possess multiple formats of the written Scriptures, it remains an essential component of the worship service.

I am often amazed at how poorly some preachers read out loud. Sometimes, getting the emphasis on the wrong word in the text shows that no thought has been given as to the sense of the passage; other times, adding words that are not there shows scant disregard for the sacredness of Scripture. After all, the very last thing the Bible warns us about is adding to or subtracting from the Scriptures: "I warn everyone who hears the words of the prophecy of this book:

if anyone adds to them, God will add to him the plagues described in this book, and if anyone takes away from the words of the book of this prophecy, God will take away his share in the tree of life and in the holy city, which are described in this book" (Rev. 22:18–19).

Exhortation

The Greek word for "exhort" is *parakaleō*. It is a very important word, and it is used in a very technical manner in Scripture. It is a word associated with the Holy Spirit and has a specific meaning when used in association with worship. It is the word that is variously translated as "exhort," "appeal," "comfort," or "encourage." It is the word associated with the Holy Spirit in the Upper Room Discourse when Jesus promised another "Helper" (John 14:16, 26; 15:26; 16:7). Jesus sends the Holy Spirit, our Helper and Comforter, to be with us when Jesus Himself is absent from us bodily.

In the same way, sermons should bring the message home by way of "helping" us *do* the requisite response to what has been taught. It is not enough that we understand in our heads what the passage is saying; the truth must have hands and feet. It must move us into action. That is not to say that the exhortation is the *only* application of a sermon. Truth is application—it is application to the mind because we need to change our ideas. Truth can and often is a form of epistemological repentance, clearing our minds of bad thinking and establishing new ways of seeing something. But "truth … accords with godliness (Titus 1:1).

John Broadus makes the same point: "Preaching is essentially a personal encounter, in which the preacher's will is making a claim through the truth upon the will of the hearer. If there is no summons, there is no sermon."[7]

John Stott cites R.W. Dale's words about the application of Jonathan Edwards in his preaching: "In the elaborate doctrinal part of Edwards' sermons, the great preacher was only getting his guns into position; but in his applications, he opened fire on the enemy. There are too many of us, I am afraid, who take so much time getting our guns into position that we have to finish without firing a shot."[8]

Teaching

Interestingly, the application (exhortation) comes before teaching in the word order of this verse. Practically, the teaching must come first, or else we are not sure what the application is. Preaching must also include teaching (Greek *didaskalia*, 1 Tim. 4:13, 16). The preacher—the sermon—must unpack the truth or truths contained in the passage. He must ask how these truths fit with other truths elsewhere in Scripture. He must demonstrate how truth in Scripture can often appear at odds with contemporary culture. There are two different worlds in view—the biblical world and the world we live in—and these two horizons must address one another.

Sermons, then, do not accommodate to the whims of modern ideas or ponderings of a congregation for more amusing, lighter discourses. The preacher is about the most serious matter of all—*the truth*. And only a knowledge of the truth can save us. Only the truth can deliver us from this evil world.

Sermons should be doctrinal. Indeed, the word "teaching" is translated "doctrines" in Matthew 15:9 and Mark 7:7. And earlier in 1 Timothy 4, it is again rendered "doctrine": "If you put these things before the brothers, you will be a good servant of Christ Jesus, being trained in the words of the faith and of the good *doctrine* that you have followed" (v. 6, emphasis added).

A preacher who does not preach doctrinally is not preaching at all.

Perseverance in Preaching

No doubt Timothy felt the burden of responsibility a heavy one. Paul adds, "Do not neglect the gift you have, which was given you by prophecy when the council of elders laid their hands on you" (1 Tim. 4:14). Preachers are human beings—frail and prone to yield under pressure to conform. Timothy's ordination was a public matter. They had laid hands on him and set him apart for the work of the gospel ministry. The Apostle and the Ephesian elders had recognized a spiritual gift for ministry and had duly confirmed Timothy's call in a public display of solemn consecration and commitment.

Too often, young preachers "burn out" for a variety of reasons. Sometimes the opposition gets to be too much. Sometimes the burden of responsibility is overbearing. But preachers must not give up. And congregations must cultivate the art of encouraging a young preacher to be faithful. I cannot emphasize enough how encouraged I have been by a kind word at the door or a thoughtful note in the mail about something I said in a sermon (that frankly I sometimes have no memory of saying!).

And then Paul adds, "Practice these things, immerse yourself in them, so that all may see your progress" (1 Tim. 4:15). Preachers need a single-mindedness in preaching. Truthfully, when I am preaching two or three sermons a week (and sometimes more), it is vital to remain fresh and disciplined. That involves a discipline with time and resources. If the sermons are to rise to a certain level of effectiveness, even for gifted preachers, there has to be constant input. That means study and hard work. Yes, the accusation that preachers only work "one day a week," or that they are visible one day a week and invisible on the other six, is sometimes said in jest. But the truth is that sermons require hard work and preachers need to study. The church should insist that the preacher's load isn't such that preparation time is minimized. It is more than reasonable that a certain portion of each workday be devoted wholly to study.

Preachers grow in their skill just as doctors and lawyers advance in their trades. The proficiencies that are acquired, the information that is absorbed, and the experience that is gained enable a preacher to grow in his craft. His "progress" (Greek *prokopē*) should be evident to all" (1 Tim. 4:15).

The Berean Spirit

When Paul preached in Berea, Luke describes their response this way: "They received the word with all eagerness, examining the Scriptures daily to see if these things were so" (Acts 17:11).

There is a duty to preach well and there is a duty to *listen* well. For this reason, I sometimes pray publicly before the sermon the words found in the collection of the martyr Thomas Cranmer (1489–1556) for the second Sunday of Advent:

> Blessed Lord, which hast caused all holy Scripture to be written for our learning; grant us that we may in such wise hear them, read, mark, learn, and inwardly digest them; that by patience and comfort of thy holy word, we may embrace, and ever hold fast the blessed hope of everlasting life, which thou has given us in our savior Jesus Christ.[9]

To rightly read, mark, learn, and inwardly digest, we must be good listeners. I am blessed at First Presbyterian Church, Columbia, to have a congregation that listens well. Nothing is more encouraging to a preacher than to see all eyes looking in his direction and a stillness in which one can hear the proverbial pin drop.

How can we become better listeners to sermons? Allow me to make some suggestions.

Listen with an expectation that God is addressing you. He will be teaching you and correcting you. Peter exhorts preachers in the early church to preach with authority: "Whoever speaks, as one who speaks oracles of God" (1 Peter 4:11). Equally, listeners should listen in a manner that suggests God is speaking through this sermon. "Speak, LORD, for your servant hears" (1 Sam. 3:9–10).

Listen intelligently. The Bereans checked whether what was said was in accord with their general understanding of the rest of Scripture. That does not imply an overly critical spirit. Rather, it suggests a mind that is active, concentrating on what is being said, following the thought process from one sentence to the next. If it helps, take notes for consideration again at a later time. Most importantly, listen to see if what is being said actually comes out of the text.

Listen for the "so what" aspect of the sermon. As James exhorts, "Be doers of the word, and not hearers only" (James 1:22). Remember that Jesus warns of those who hear the Word but immediately forget it. The seed sown in good soil "are those who, hearing the word, hold it fast in an honest and good heart, and bear fruit with patience" (Luke 8:15).

6

The Offering

Are New Testament Christians expected to tithe?
It's a tricky question, and one that cannot be answered with a simple yes or no. One can argue, for example, that the tithe was mandated under the old covenant to support the Levites (Num. 18:21–24). Failure to tithe is referred to as "robbing" God (Mal. 3:6–12). But when we come to the New Testament, there is no express command to tithe.[1] Are we then to conclude that Christians are free to give nothing at all? Not so fast!

The only passage in the New Testament that suggests that Christians are expected to tithe is Jesus' encounter with the Pharisees who were insisting on tithing spices and had entered into a legalistic interpretation of the law. There, Jesus says: "Woe to you, scribes and Pharisees, hypocrites! For you tithe mint and dill and cumin, and have neglected the weightier matters of the law: justice and mercy and faithfulness. These you ought to have done, without neglecting the others" (Matt. 23:23). In criticizing this crippling approach of the Pharisees, Jesus does not say that the entire concept of tithing is wrongheaded. Rather, He proposes that tithing belongs to those aspects of the law that are "less weighty." Pharisaical disdain of gentiles, for example, was a far greater sin than failing to tithe. Still, Jesus was not saying that the very concept of tithing had no place in the new covenant era.

New Testament churches were expected to give an "offering"—a *voluntary* gift for the purposes of providing aid to the poor and needy.[2] The *offering* is the subject of 1 Corinthians 16:1–4, and an extensive account is recorded in 2 Corinthians 8 and 9. The need to help the Christian poor was urgent: Christians in Jerusalem (mostly Jewish by birth) were ostracized upon becoming Christians, and many lost their livelihoods and were banished from family gatherings and support. Famine added to this burden. Paul told the Galatian church that when he first encountered James, John, and Peter in Jerusalem, they specifically asked him to "remember the poor" (Gal. 2:10). Paul took them up on this plea, spending a great deal of time in the largely gentile churches he established to raise funds for the needy Christians in Jerusalem.

The Church in Corinth

To get some understanding of why Paul addresses the issue of giving in his Corinthian letters, we should take a little time and get a clearer picture of the Corinthian church.

Paul's first visit to Corinth, during his second extensive missionary journey, is described in some detail in Acts 18. At first, he taught and preached in the synagogue. At some point he made friends with Priscilla and Aquila, probably through a mutual skill in tentmaking and working with leather goods. Priscilla and Aquila were among those Jews exiled from Rome under the edict of Emperor Claudius. We do not know if they were Christians before they arrived in

Corinth, but they most certainly were when Paul left (Acts 18:26; 1 Cor. 16:19).

Opposition made Paul nervous, and in a vision, the Lord told Paul not to be afraid but to keep on speaking. The Apostle remained for another eighteen months (Acts 18:8–11). Then trouble ensued. The synagogue leader, Sosthenes, was badly beaten up (presumably because he, too, had converted to Christianity), and days later, Paul, Priscilla, and Aquila set sail for Syria.

When Paul left, the church seems to have been significant in size, with many converted Jews as well as pagans. Paul describes having "planted" this church (1 Cor. 3:6). First Corinthians seems to have been written as much as two and a half years later from Ephesus (1 Cor. 16:8).

When Paul initially came to Corinth, the city had around one hundred thousand inhabitants.[3] Even though Corinth occupied a central part of what was otherwise Greek culture, the city itself seems to have been largely Roman. The city's architecture mimicked Rome's. The temple dedicated to the emperor, for example, was on a higher elevation than the Greek forum. Many inscriptions found in recent excavations are in Latin rather than Greek.

The city included a larger than usual number of freedmen, onetime slaves who had been emancipated, most of whom arrived straight from Rome itself.[4] The implication we derive from reading the Corinthians letters is that Corinth was relatively prosperous. The city welcomed entrepreneurs like Paul, Priscilla, and Aquila. "It was no doubt a place where fortunes were made by some and lost by others, all contributing to a complex world in which social status took on great importance."[5] When Paul writes his letter to the Romans from Corinth, he sends greetings from some of the city officials, including

Erastus, the city treasurer (Rom. 16:23). He goes on to mention a host of others—Chloe (1 Cor. 1:11) and Fortunatus, Achaicus, and Stephanas (1 Cor. 16:17), who are thought to be among the wealthier businessmen and who had traveled to Rome and were therefore known to Christians there. Excavations of the Corinthian city square reveal small shops, and it is likely that Paul, Priscilla, and Aquila made and sold tents in a similar one.

Every two years, the city of Corinth hosted the Isthmian Games, which brought in hundreds, perhaps thousands, of people from elsewhere. Paul's use of an athlete in 1 Corinthians 9 highly suggests that he was in the city when one of these events took place.

Divisions and Problems

The reason Paul writes is partly made obvious in the first chapter. There were divisions between various factions identified as followers of Paul, Peter, and Apollos, and Christ, the latter suggesting a group that had abandoned all three men (1 Cor. 1:12).

The church in Corinth was troubled by additional problems: sexual sin, which threatened the *E* word, *excommunication*—"Purge the evil person from among you" (5:13); a strange issue of asceticism, resulting in some who were saying, "It is good for a man not to have sexual relations with a woman" (7:1); conscience issues that led to accusations from weak Christians that eating meat offered to idols was sinful, resulting in Paul's laying down a principle: "Eat whatever is sold in the meat market without raising any question on the ground of conscience" (10:25; cf. 8:4–10); unbelievable acts of thoughtlessness and selfishness at the Lord's Supper (11:17–34); the use of Apostolic sign-gifts of tongues and prophecy (chs. 12–14), necessitating Paul to write the extraordinarily beautiful chapter about love (ch. 13); and confusion about what happens after death (ch. 15).

As Paul draws 1 Corinthians to a close, he reminds the Corinthians (to whom he has spoken severely about issues involving selfishness) that others—particularly in Jerusalem—are quite literally starving. That fact should help focus their thoughts and remind them of what is important. *Money* is how the epistle ends. When Paul arrives, he wants this collection to be ready. He doesn't want to have to engage in some unseemly harangue for shekels.

Is it strategic that this is what closes this lengthy, disturbing letter? Yes, I think it is. Something was radically wrong in Corinth. The church displayed a systemic abuse of gospel freedom that made them behave in outrageously selfish ways. They were, frankly, self-absorbed. All the many problems that troubled this church stem from a failure of generosity.

The cure? *Giving!* More particularly, giving to others in need. And it should be done decently and in order. They were to set aside an offering for the poor in Jerusalem on the first day of every week— the day known as the Lord's Day, the day that replaced the Jewish Sabbath. And although the text does not specifically mention it, it seems reasonable to conclude that the offering was gathered when they met for worship.

The collection was for the church in Jerusalem. In Acts 15, at the Jerusalem Council, stresses and strains emerged in the ongoing relationship between the Jewish Christians and the gentile churches that Paul was planting. One of the conclusions they reached is referred to in Galatians: "Only, they asked us to remember the poor, the very thing I was eager to do" (2:10).

Principles of Giving

The Corinthian epistles do not specifically command that the offering for Jerusalem be set aside during the course of the worship service. And historically, according to Hughes Oliphant Old, there is no record of its inclusion in Reformed worship until much later.[6] The list of the elements of worship in the Westminster Confession remarkably does not include a collection or offering.[7]

In the first seventeen years of my ministry at a Presbyterian church in Belfast, Northern Ireland, there was no collection or offering during the service. Two boxes, one on either side of the entrance doorway, were fixed to the back wall, and people gave as they entered the sanctuary.[8] Today, however, in the vast majority of churches, the offering is a standard feature of public worship.

Limiting ourselves to the passages in 1 and 2 Corinthians, what principles guide us in giving?

First, the offering was *voluntary*. Paul makes it clear: "I say this not as a command, but to prove by the earnestness of others that your love also is genuine" (2 Cor. 8:8). "Each one must give as he has decided in his heart, not reluctantly or under compulsion, for God loves a cheerful giver" (2 Cor. 9:7).

The voluntary nature of the offering is hinted at by the word Paul uses in 1 Corinthians 16:1: "the collection" (Greek *logeia*). It is not used anywhere else when Paul is addressing the issue. Elsewhere he employs a variety of terms: "gift" (or "grace"; Greek *charis*, 1 Cor. 16:3), "relief" (2 Cor. 8:4), "ministry" (2 Cor. 9:1, 12–13).

The possible reason for the use of the word *logeia* is that the word originates in Corinth. It was *their* word for what Paul was asking for. The word was sometimes used for an irregular form of taxation. Perhaps the Corinthians were skeptical of this redistribution of money, and Paul took the word and poured a new meaning into it. Thereafter, he does not use the word again. What he has in mind is not a tax—something that is given because it is demanded with threats of punitive damages if refused. No, Paul wants them to give voluntarily.

Second, giving is *a reflex of the love of Christ for us*. In 2 Corinthians, he elaborates on this matter, suggesting that giving is an "overflow" (8:2; 9:12). The grace of the Lord Jesus Christ had so filled their souls that it overflowed in acts of kindness to others.

Paul draws attention to the generosity of the northern church in Macedonia: "We want you to know, brothers, about the grace of God that has been given among the churches of Macedonia, for in a severe test of affliction, their abundance of joy and their extreme poverty have overflowed in a wealth of generosity on their part. For they gave according to their means, as I can testify, and beyond their means, of their own accord, begging us earnestly for the favor of taking part in the relief of the saints" (2 Cor. 8:1–4). Though these northern churches were themselves poor, they begged to be included and gave until it hurt. Then Paul makes his move on the Corinthians: "See that you excel in this act of grace also" (2 Cor. 8:7). It is as if Paul were saying, "Don't let those northern churches make you look stingy!"

To underline the gracious aspect of giving, Paul employs the most massive theological justification he can think of—the love of Christ for His people: "For you know the grace of our Lord Jesus Christ, that though he was rich, yet for your sake he became poor, so that you by his poverty might become rich" (2 Cor. 8:9). Give in a Jesus-like manner, sacrificially.

Third, giving *demonstrates our love for one another*. In chapter 13 of 1 Corinthians, Paul wrote one of the most eloquent expressions of love in all of literature. "If I have all faith, so as to remove mountains, but have not love, I am nothing" (v. 2). And in chapter 16, the matter of demonstrating love rises to the surface once more:

Let all that you do be done in love. (v. 14)

If anyone has no love for the Lord, let him be accursed. (v. 22)

My love be with you all in Christ Jesus. (v. 24)

And when he returns to the issue in 2 Corinthians, he makes it a test of *genuineness*: "So give proof before the churches of your love" (8:24).

Fourth, giving must be done *cheerfully*: "God loves a cheerful [lit. "hilarious"] giver" (9:7).

God loves it when His children are overflowing in happiness in their giving. As a parent is overjoyed when a son or daughter makes something and presents it as a gift, even if the gift (in itself) is nothing much to speak about. The joy in giving stems from a heart that is filled with gospel grace. "It is more blessed to give than to receive" (Acts 20:35).

Fifth, the responsibility for giving is laid upon *everyone*: "Each of you is to put something aside and store it up" (1 Cor. 16:2). There would have been exceptions, of course—those who were unemployed and those in Corinth who were themselves in financial difficulties. Even so, the widow's mite is an act of immense generosity that the Lord does not overlook (Mark 12:41–44; Luke 21:1–4).

It was important to my wife and me that our children learn the rhythm of weekly giving at a young age. They were encouraged to put in a coin or two from their pocket money, so as to experience the joy of giving early in life.

Jon Payne writes:

> Don't let the placing of your tithe and/or offering in the collection plate during the worship service be a mere formality or a mindless ritual. Rather, as with the other parts of the liturgy, make it a conscious, joyful act of worship. One way to do this is to bow your head after placing your offering in the plate and say a prayer of thanksgiving for God's abundant faithfulness, also declaring your trust in Him to continue to provide your daily bread.[9]

Sixth, our giving *expresses God's glory*. Paul tells the Corinthians that giving "will glorify God" (2 Cor. 9:13). How does this happen? It all depends on whether you view God as One who "takes" or One who "gives." Behind the picture of cheerful giving lies a heart that sees God as the abundant Supplier, the generous Giver, the bountiful Helper. When you see God like that, the "ask" is not so much a command as a joy.

Weekly giving to help the Lord's work is a vital element of godliness and a proper aspect of worship.

7

Prayer

Think of a typical Sunday morning worship service with which you are familiar. What percentage of the service is taken up with prayer? Is it an unfair question? I do not think so.

Far too many church services include only one or two short prayers. The pastoral prayer—that section of the service where the minister prays a lengthy prayer over a range of issues—has almost disappeared in many present-day services, so much so that when a friend reintroduced a lengthy pastoral prayer, an elder complained that the pastoral prayer had lasted "seven minutes and forty-three seconds." He had actually timed the prayer because he thought it was far too long! Clearly, among other matters, he was unfamiliar with Presbyterian liturgical history.

Typically, there are five specific prayers in a traditional Presbyterian service.

The first comes at the very beginning and is usually referred to as the *invocation*. The word *invocation* comes from the Latin *invocare*, "to invoke, to call on." Its purpose is very specific (though many pastors fail to understand it). It is to call upon God to "come down" and bless the worship that follows. Typically, they are composed of a few short sentences. Here is a well-known prayer from John Chrysostom:

Almighty God, who has given us grace at this time with one accord to make our common supplications unto You and does promise that when two or three are gathered together in Your name You will grant their requests; fulfill now, O Lord, the desires and petitions of Your servants, as may be most expedient for them; granting us in this world knowledge of Your truth, and in the world to come life everlasting. Amen.[1]

Another prayer that is often included in the liturgy is the corporate recitation of the Lord's Prayer.[2] Presbyterian and Reformed traditions in the United Kingdom, for example, following the example of later Puritan worship, became suspicious of rote prayers, viewing them as violating Jesus' warning in the Sermon on the Mount: "And when you pray, do not heap up empty phrases as the Gentiles do, for they think that they will be heard for their many words" (Matt. 6:7). Vain repetition *may* lead to formalism, but repetition done with a sincere heart need not. And, in any case, this warning is followed by the Lord's Prayer, which most Christians have recited in worship ever since.

Then comes the *prayer of confession*. These are prayed corporately in my own church, and most of them I compose myself. They emphasize the sinfulness of our hearts and the need for God's gracious forgiveness and are followed by a statement of assurance from Scripture.

Here are a couple of examples of some prayers of confession I have used:

Heavenly Father, all of us are guilty of Adam's first transgression. As our representative, when he fell, we fell with him. When he failed to present a perfect righteousness, he became utterly indisposed, disabled, and made opposite to all that is spiritually good, and wholly inclined to all evil, and that continually. From this condition proceeds all actual transgressions. This was our condition by birth, but grace found us. We discovered a Savior whose obedience was reckoned to our account. He rescued and redeemed us, and we are thankful beyond words. We have been baptized into Christ, into His death and resurrection. We bless You this morning that in Christ, we are children of God, heirs of God, and joint heirs with Jesus Christ. Amen. (Based on Westminster Larger Catechism 25)

Heavenly Father, Your Word commands us to "bear one another's burdens," for in doing so we "fulfill the law of Christ." Too often, we find ourselves wanting to focus on ourselves rather than others. We have problems, too, and sometimes we just want to wallow in self-pity. Lord, You know how often we have had pity parties in these last few weeks. We are truly sorry. Help us to look outside of ourselves, to reach out to our brothers and sisters and neighbors and see how we can help them. Help us to pray for one another, regularly. And grant us the joy of knowing that all our sins are covered by the blood of Jesus. Amen. (Based on Gal. 6:2)

Yet another prayer in the liturgy is the *pastoral prayer*. It is the longest of all the prayers, and it typically contains formal exaltation of God in His triune majesty, thanksgiving for the gospel, and specific petitions on behalf of the congregation (and sometimes individuals),[3] the worldwide church, and the nation. Some pastors write them out beforehand and read them during the service. My own habit has been to meditate on what I will pray for beforehand but to pray them extemporaneously.

Illumination

Another liturgical prayer that can be identified is the prayer that comes before the sermon and is typically called the *prayer of illumination*. This prayer also is a very specific prayer asking for the help of the Holy Spirit to rightly understand the Scriptures and heed its application. Like the invocation, it is short. Liturgically, it is sometimes referred to as an epiclesis (though it is not the only occasion where this term may be applied). This name derives from the Greek word *epiklēsis*, or its verb form, *epikalein*, "to call upon, summon." John Calvin gave specific attention to the way that the Holy Spirit *illuminates* Scripture, helping the reader, through the right use of means (commentaries, sermons, etc.), to rightly understand its teaching.[4] I mentioned in the previous chapter Thomas Cranmer's prayer of illumination. Here is another I have often used, one that I wrote myself:

> Lord, we are poor and needy, and in need of being fed. Help me to rightly divide the Word of Truth and grant us all ears to hear. Speak, Lord, for Your servant is listening. In Jesus' name. Amen.

A House of Prayer

We saw earlier the importance of Luke's summary of the early church in Acts 2: "And they devoted themselves to the apostles' teaching and the fellowship, to the breaking of bread and the prayers" (v. 42). The use of the definite article (*the* prayers) suggests an ordered liturgy most likely dependent on the synagogue liturgy.

It is of paramount importance to note that the central feature of temple worship in the Old Testament was prayer. The temple, as Solomon's lengthy prayer at the time of the dedication of the temple makes clear, is first of all a house of prayer (1 Kings 8:23–61). And Jesus underlines the fact, citing Isaiah's allusion that His "house shall be called a house of prayer" (Isa. 56:7; cf. Matt. 21:13). As Hughes Oliphant Old puts it, "The Temple is dedicated as a house of prayer to which Israel may come in time of drought, in time of famine, in time of military defeat, and in time of personal disaster."[5]

After the destruction of Solomon's temple and the establishment of the exilic synagogue to compensate for Israel's inability to access Jerusalem and its temple, prayer once again becomes a central feature. Different times and different settings meant that "the prayer of the synagogue developed in a very different way from the prayer of the Temple."[6] The central prayer of the synagogue was the Amida or, as it is sometimes called, the Eighteen Benedictions. We can be fairly certain that this was the pattern of prayer that Jesus and His disciples employed. And what is interesting is that the Amida was not a liturgical form set in stone but one that provided the subjects or topics or themes upon which a rabbi would extemporize.

The Amida consisted of three benedictions of praise and thanksgiving, followed by six supplications of a more personal nature, six petitions for the well-being of Israel, and finally three further benedictions of praise and thanksgiving that led to the Aaronic benediction.

Like the Amida, the Lord's Prayer (particularly in its longer form, which includes the ending "For thine is the kingdom, the power and the glory, forever"[7]) begins and ends with praise.

An examination of the central emphases of the Lord's Prayer will help us understand the shape and contours of liturgical prayer and help understand how to pray. After all, all the prayers offered are *our* prayers, and we should be ready to underline the "Amen" that concludes each of these prayers as our personal affirmation.

Michael Horton draws attention to an alarming feature of much present-day worship—the absence of prayer: "One of the most disappointing features of contemporary worship is the absence of prayer, and one suspects that few of the youth in evangelical mainline churches today even know the Lord's Prayer, which covenant children have prayed—and used as a model for their prayers—for two thousand years. If corporate prayer does not play an important part in our worship, it should not be surprising that it is marginalized in the individual lives of Christians."[8]

Horton is right in suggesting that there is an important link between public prayers heard during the worship service and private, personal prayers prayed at home. Putting it positively, public prayers will help shape how individuals pray in private and in the home. "Pray then like this," Jesus said (Matt. 6:9).

Prayer Produces a Sense of Awe

Strong, effective praying in the liturgy of public worship is bound to have an impact for good. After his summary description of the early church in Acts 2, including the reference to "the prayers" (v. 42), Luke adds, "and awe came upon every soul" (v. 43). Prayer brought a sense of the seriousness of public worship. Worshipers were held captive by a sense of God's glory and holiness.

R. Kent Hughes quotes from Samuel Miller's book *Thoughts on Public Prayer*:

When the heart is engaged, and in proportion that it is deeply and warmly engaged; when the value of spiritual things is cordially felt, and the attainment of them earnestly desired; when the soul has a heartfelt sense of its own unworthiness, and an humble, tender confidence in the Saviour's love and grace—in a word, when the whole soul is prepared to flow out in accordance with the language uttered, in faith, love, gratitude and heavenly desire;—then, and only then, will every portion, and word, and tone be, in some good degree, in happy keeping with the nature and scope of the exercise.[9]

Hughes then goes on to list a number of conclusions from Miller's thoughts, addressed particularly to pastors. I have both elaborated and changed them to reflect the perspective of the person in the pew:

- We need pastors who have deep, regular, private communion with God. This will be evident to most from the manner and content of the public prayers of the pastor.
- We need pastors who are authentic in the manner that they pray, reflecting the appropriate feeling as they pray.
- Public prayers from the pulpit must not be lectures addressed at the congregation. We need to sense that the preacher's words are our words, too, addressed to our Father in heaven.
- We need pastors who convey that they have genuinely searched their own hearts before walking into the pulpit.[10]

For my part, I have been ambivalent about "reading" pastoral prayers written out in advance, though many of my colleagues do this routinely. To help me in the moment, I often scribble some thoughts about the direction of the prayer. Extemporaneous pastoral prayers can too easily have a sameness about them, when ministers use the same language over and over. When this occurs, perhaps the minister should write out his prayers beforehand to ensure a sufficient variety and freshness in his public prayer.

8

Creeds:
What Do You Believe?

*C*redo in Deum . . . I believe in God.

These words (in English) form a part of our regular Sunday morning worship at First Presbyterian Church, Columbia, a creed that is recited by the entire congregation. They are the opening words of the Apostles' Creed. The word *creed* is derived from the Latin verb *credo*, meaning "I believe." A "creed" is therefore quite simply a statement of truths that we believe to be true.

I often think that when I hear a thousand people recite the Apostles' Creed in unison on a Sunday morning, it must surely be the most countercultural moment in North America. It isolates us from current worldviews as it connects us to the countless believers who have recited it for generations.[1] Across the theological spectrum, the Apostles' Creed has long been cherished as a trustworthy summary of the Christian faith.

There are other, earlier examples of creedal (catechetical) material, some of which are found in the Bible itself. In the first generation or two after Pentecost, before a New Testament canon existed, candidates for baptism, most of whom would have been adults as the church moved into new territory, were urged to memorize short statements of faith. Philippians 2:5–11 and Colossians 1:15–23, for example, are thought to be examples of early catechetical statements.

The so-called five faithful sayings in Paul's letters are also examples of early statements of faith (1 Tim. 1:12–17; 3:1–7; 4:8–10; 2 Tim. 2:11–13; Titus 3:1–8). A summary of Christian belief was therefore both useful and necessary to familiarize young believers with essential doctrines of the Christian faith.

Some traditions within Puritan and Reformed worship voiced disagreement with the use of creeds in liturgy, especially when statements are made that go further than what might be deemed as basic Christian truth. An example might be the Westminster Confession's statement on election, for example. Is it a requirement of every Christian in membership at a local church to affirm this truth? Presbyterians, for example, have traditionally required subscription to the Westminster Confession only by office bearers and ministers. And perhaps because of this, and because of a desire to implement a stricter application of the regulative principle, some conservative traditions, particularly in the United Kingdom, have moved away from the use of creeds in the liturgy altogether (including the Apostles' Creed). Nevertheless, Reformed worship historically has widely endorsed the use of creedal statements, particularly the Apostles' Creed.

The Apostles' Creed

Several versions of the Apostles' Creed (ancient and modern) exist, but the one we employ in our own church is the version in the traditional (early modern) English:

I believe in God the Father Almighty, Maker of heaven and earth.

And in Jesus Christ His only Son our Lord; who was conceived by the Holy Ghost, born of the Virgin Mary, suffered under Pontius Pilate, was crucified, dead, and buried; He descended into hell; the third day He rose again from the dead; He ascended into heaven, and sitteth on the right hand of God the Father Almighty; from thence He shall come to judge the quick and the dead.

I believe in the Holy Ghost; the holy catholic Church; the communion of saints; the forgiveness of sins; the resurrection of the body; and the life everlasting.

Amen.

Yes, we still say "sitteth," largely because almost everyone recalls it from memory. Arguments for using modern English (replacing the personal pronouns *thee, thou,* and *thine*) are more than valid, but in a congregation where a learned pattern of behavior has existed for generations, it would be difficult and, in my view, unnecessary to make the congregation relearn the creed.

Far more importantly, what does the Apostles' Creed teach us? In short answer, it teaches us *seven* basic truths.

First and foremost, it teaches us the importance of the doctrine of the Trinity.

I believe in God the Father Almighty . . .
And in Jesus Christ, His only begotten Son, our Lord . . .
I believe in the Holy Ghost . . .

The doctrine of the Trinity was affirmed at the Council of Nicaea in AD 325 and later expanded at the Council of Constantinople in

AD 381 to include a particular statement about the Holy Spirit. A careful reading of the Niceno-Constantinopolitan Creed reveals a remarkable similarity in shape and language to the Apostles' Creed:

I believe in one God, the Father Almighty, Maker of heaven and earth, and of all things visible and invisible.

And in one Lord Jesus Christ, the only-begotten Son of God, begotten of the Father before all worlds; God of God, Light of Light, very God of very God; begotten, not made, being of one substance with the Father, by whom all things were made.

Who, for us men for our salvation, came down from heaven, and was incarnate by the Holy Spirit of the virgin Mary, and was made man; and was crucified also for us under Pontius Pilate; He suffered and was buried; and the third day He rose again, according to the Scriptures; and ascended into heaven, and sits on the right hand of the Father; and He shall come again, with glory, to judge the quick and the dead; whose kingdom shall have no end.

And I believe in the Holy Ghost, the Lord and Giver of Life; who proceeds from the Father [and the Son]; who with the Father and the Son together is worshiped and glorified; who spoke by the prophets.

And I believe in one holy catholic and apostolic Church. I acknowledge one baptism for the remission of sins; and I look for the resurrection of the dead, and the life of the world to come. Amen.

The doctrine of the Trinity is vital to the shape of the gospel. Yes, the doctrine of the Trinity is *that* important. After all, what precisely *is* the gospel? Is it not a statement of the substitutionary atoning death of God the Son, a sacrifice that is made effective and applied in the life of a believer by the power of God the Holy Spirit, and all in fulfillment of the will of God the Father?

The unfolding revelation of the Trinitarian nature of the being of God in the Bible is like a detective story. Clues are given that initially have little or no significance, but in hindsight, when all the clues are assembled together, a certain narrative is assembled. As the reader progresses through the unfolding stages of the plot, one is forced to go back to the beginning and capture added significance to aspects of the story that at first proved strange and puzzling.[2] The fact that in the opening chapter of Scripture God uses the second person plural to describe the way that Adam and Eve were created, "Let *us* make man . . ." (Gen. 1:26, emphasis added), seems very significant. Or the even more puzzling fact that the Hebrew for "god" (*Elohim*) is in a plural form. By itself, these grammatical uses did not lead the Jews to interpret these things as evidence of plurality. Rather, they viewed them as examples of regal majesty (as when Queen Victoria would refer to herself saying, "*We* are not amused").

However, as the pages of Scripture turn from Malachi to Matthew, things become clearer. With the benefit of hindsight, clues are clarified. No one makes a bolder comment than the Apostle John: "In the beginning was the Word, and the Word was with God, and the Word was God. He was in the beginning with God. All things were made through him, and without him was not any thing made that was made. . . . And the Word became flesh and dwelt among us" (John 1:1–3, 14). The Creator-God who made all things at the beginning—described in Genesis 1—was Jesus. Jesus is God, but He is not the only one who is the one God. The Father is God and the Son is God. And there remains only one God.

Similarly, Jesus, in pronouncing the church's mandate to go and make disciples of all the nations of the world, mentions the sacramental sign and seal of the gospel—baptism—which is to be done "in the name of the Father and of the Son and of the Holy Spirit" (Matt. 28:19). Note that the name is in the singular, not the plural: the *one* name of the Father, Son, and Holy Spirit. Three-personed God: Father, Son, and Holy Spirit. Each person of the Trinity has a role to play in the fulfillment of the external operations of God—that is, in creation, redemption, and judgment. For example, notice how carefully Paul delineates the work of Father, Son, and Holy Spirit in the provision and application of redemption to the people of God (the elect) in Ephesians 1:

> Blessed be the *God and Father* of our Lord Jesus Christ, who has blessed us in Christ with every spiritual blessing in the heavenly places, even as he chose us in him before the foundation of the world, that we should be holy and blameless before him. In love he predestined us for adoption to himself as sons *through Jesus Christ*, according to the purpose of his will, to the praise of his glorious grace, with which he has blessed us in the Beloved. *In him* [Jesus Christ] we have redemption through his blood, the forgiveness of our trespasses, according to the riches of his grace, which he lavished upon us, in all wisdom and insight making known to us the mystery of his will, according to his purpose, which he set forth in Christ as a plan for the fullness of time, to unite all things in him, things in heaven and things on earth.
>
> In him we have obtained an inheritance, having been predestined according to the purpose of him who works all things according to the counsel of his will, so that we who were the first to

hope in Christ might be to the praise of his glory. In him you also, when you heard the word of truth, the gospel of your salvation, and believed in him, were sealed with *the promised Holy Spirit*, who is the guarantee of our inheritance until we acquire possession of it, to the praise of his glory. (vv. 3–14, emphasis added)

It is impossible to outline the gospel apart from an explicit reference to the way that all three persons of the Trinity have a role to play in our salvation. Therefore, whenever we address God in prayer, we do so by employing the same formula: we speak to the Father, through the mediation of the Son, and by the help of the Holy Spirit. Prayer, like the gospel, is shaped by the Trinity. Without the doctrine of the Trinity, we have Unitarianism. And Unitarianism is not Christianity. It is a heresy.

Creation

Second, the Apostles' Creed emphasizes the importance of the doctrine of *creation*. "I believe in God the Father Almighty, *Maker of heaven and earth*." Several matters are highlighted in brief compass. There is the truth that all that exists—in heaven and earth, unseen and seen, spiritual and material—apart from God Himself, comes into being and is sustained in being by the sovereign will of God. The material universe is not eternal. The cosmos does not owe its existence to eternal matter (a gas, a molecule, a force). Perhaps, as has been said many times, the most profound question that we can ask is this: Why is there something and not nothing? And the possible answers are few:

- One possible answer is to suggest that before there was something, there was *something*. There has always existed a force of some kind—electromagnetism, or gravity perhaps. Or perhaps a single proton existed. And from it comes an explosion, and the rest is history. Of course, there is still the dilemma as to where this *something* came from.

- Another possibility is that before there was something, there was *nothing*. Nothing produces everything. I think we need to repeat that last sentence several times in our heads to get a sense of how absurd it is.

- Another alternative, the Christian worldview, is that God created the universe in which we live. Every atom, subatomic particle, and force is the result of God's handiwork. "Let there be . . . ," and there was! And the creation continues (despite the curse that has come upon it due to the fall) to reflect God's eternal power and deity (Ps. 19; Rom. 1:20). No single human being may claim ignorance of this fact: humanity is "without excuse" (Rom. 1:20). The doctrine of creation provides us with a way of understanding *who* we are and what we are made *for*. We were made in God's image and after His likeness (Gen. 1:26–27). That means we have a moral and spiritual identity, a responsibility to live as redeemed individuals for His glory, to reflect His image. It provides us with a way of defining sexuality, purpose, motivation, aspiration, and much more. Likewise, knowing that the world is created by God prevents us from viewing it as something essentially evil. Evil exists within creation. The world is out of joint and travails in pain (Rom. 8:22–24). Terrible disasters ruin the lives of many, and these are to be viewed as birth pangs as creation awaits its own redemption (Rom. 8:19–20). However, even in its fallen state, creation is to be enjoyed, its resources harnessed for the good of humanity as man exercises lordship over the world God has made. Creation is good in God's eyes (Gen. 1:31), and it should look so in ours (1 Tim. 4:4).

The Incarnation

Third, the Apostles' Creed teaches the importance of the incarnation—the life, death, burial, resurrection, and ascension of Jesus Christ. It is a comprehensive statement that signals the importance not just of the cross-work of Christ but of His birth of the Virgin Mary. Jesus was truly human in every way, apart from sin. But His human origin was entirely unique. The fallen world needed a Savior but could not produce one. His human nature was the creation of the Holy Spirit in the Virgin's womb. Later creedal statements would specify that the creation of the human flesh of Jesus was not *ex nihilo* (out of nothing) but *ex Maria*, taking (in modern terms) DNA directly from the Virgin. Thus, Jesus is the last Adam, the second man, come to do what we cannot: provide full and complete obedience to the law and take the sinner's place as God's representative agent.

The Apostles' Creed traces the trajectory of Jesus' human life from conception to ascension, emphasizing His *suffering, death*, and *burial*. One statement has troubled the church, more so in recent times than in the past—the "descent into hell" clause (*descendit in inferno*). Did Jesus actually descend into hell? Could such a holy form be found in such a place? The problem relates to the meaning of the word *hell* that has solidified since this creed was originally written (or translated into English). J.I. Packer explains it succinctly:

> The English is misleading, for "hell" has changed its sense since the English form of the Creed was fixed. Originally "hell" meant the place of the departed as such, corresponding to the Greek *Hades* and the Hebrew *Sheol*. That is what it means here, where the Creed echoes Peter's statement that Psalm 16:10, "thou wilt not abandon my soul to *Hades*" (so RSV: AV has "hell"), was a prophecy fulfilled when Jesus rose (see Acts 2:27–31). But since the seventeenth century, "hell" has been used to signify only the state of final retribution for the godless, for which the New Testament name is *Gehenna*.
>
> What the Creed means, however, is that Jesus entered, not *Gehenna*, but *Hades*—that is, that he really died, and that it was from a genuine death, not a simulated one, that he rose.
>
> Perhaps it should be said (though one shrinks from laboring something so obvious) that "descended" does *not* imply that the way from Palestine to Hades is down into the ground, any more than "rose" implies that Jesus returned to surface level up the equivalent of a mine shaft! The language of descent is used because Hades, being the place of the dis-embodied, is *lower* in worth and dignity than is life on earth, where body and soul are together and humanity is in that sense whole.[3]

Some have gone further in interpreting what Jesus might have accomplished during that period when His body lay in the grave and His soul or spirit was in heaven by drawing attention to the (possible) *chronological* sequence of thought in Peter's reference to Jesus' death and resurrection in 1 Peter 3. The passage is a notoriously difficult one to interpret accurately, and one commentator lists more than a dozen different possibilities![4] However, if we remove some of the more troublesome aspects of the text and simply follow the narrative of Jesus' work, we see a possible clue to its interpretation: "For Christ also suffered once for sins, the righteous for the unrighteous, that he might bring us to God, being put to death in the flesh but made alive in the spirit ... through the resurrection of Jesus Christ, who has gone into heaven and is at the right hand of God, with angels, authorities, and powers having been subjected to him" (1 Peter 3:18–22).

What is clear is that we have a sequence of actions—suffering, death, resurrection, ascension into heaven. If we now ask what happens between His death and resurrection *according to 1 Peter 3*, we have the following answer: *He preached to the spirits in prison* (v. 19). Some have therefore made the observation that in the interval from burial to resurrection (about thirty hours), Jesus proclaimed His victory over the powers of darkness, thus fulfilling a major aspect of the New Testament's understanding of the cross, summarized no more succinctly than in 1 John 3:8: "The reason the Son of God appeared was to destroy the works of the devil." Jesus came to undo the curse and, in His victory over death, proclaimed Himself the seed of the woman whose task it was to regain paradise for Adam's elect children (Gen. 3:15).

Another interpretation of the descent into hell clause is that given by John Calvin.[5] The Reformer argues that Jesus' "descent into hell" was not merely His descending into physical death and the grave. For Calvin, the sufferings of Jesus were the kind of sufferings a tormented soul in hell would experience. Thus, on the cross, He endured the pains of hell. He "bore all the punishments [evildoers] ought to have sustained" with only one exception, that those torments could not keep hold of him forever. He "suffered the death that God in his wrath had inflicted upon the wicked." Calvin goes on: "Not only that Christ's body was given as the price of our redemption, but that he paid a greater and more excellent price in suffering in his soul the terrible torments of a condemned and forsaken man. . . . Surely no more terrible abyss can be conceived than to feel yourself forsaken and estranged from God; and when you call upon him, not to be heard. It is as if God himself had plotted your ruin."[6]

The Holy Spirit

Fourth, the Apostles' Creed focuses on the Holy Spirit, though it is without nuance and amplification (a mere statement of belief in the Holy Spirit). Unfortunately, the use of "Holy Ghost" in the version we employ at our own church adds to the confusion and mystery Christians associate with the Holy Spirit. The Holy Spirit is *not* an apparition of a dead person!

The location of the statement about the Holy Spirit is deeply significant. In putting the statement immediately after the statement on the work of Christ, it resonates with Augustinian and Reformation understanding of the work of the Holy Spirit in applying all that Christ has accomplished on our behalf. Few statements are clearer about the role of the Holy Spirit in the application of redemption than the one that starts book 3 of John Calvin's *Institutes*:

We must now examine this question. How do we receive those benefits which the Father bestowed on his only-begotten Son— not for Christ's own private use, but that he might enrich poor and needy men? First, we must understand that as long as Christ remains outside of us, and we are separated from him, all that he has suffered and done for the salvation of the human race remains useless and of no value to us. Therefore, to share with us what he has received from the Father, he had to become ours and to dwell within us. For this reason, he is called "our Head" [Eph. 4:15], and "the first-born among many brethren" [Rom. 8:29]. We also, in turn, are said to be "engrafted into him" [Rom. 11:17], and to "put on Christ" [Gal. 3:27]; for, as I have said, all that he possesses is nothing to us until we grow into one body with him. It is true that we can obtain this by faith. Yet since we see that not all indiscriminately embrace that communion with Christ which is offered through the gospel, reason itself teaches us to climb higher and to examine into the secret energy of the Spirit, by which we come to enjoy Christ and all of his benefits.[7]

From calling to regeneration to sanctification—both in its initial declarative sense whereby we are declared to be "holy" (or "saints"— i.e., "holy ones") through faith in Christ (cf. 1 Cor. 1:1–2) and in our final translation to glory—the operative agent is the Holy Spirit, Christ's personal representative agent on earth, the "other" Helper promised by Jesus in the upper room (John 14:16, 26; 15:26; 16:7).

The Church

Fifth, and crucially, the Apostles' Creed declares our belief in Christ's church—the holy catholic church. *Catholic* here does not mean Roman Catholic (the visible institution known as the Roman Catholic Church had yet to manifest itself when the creed first appeared). *Catholic* means the universal, worldwide church, spatially and temporally. Jesus' church stretches back over centuries and continues until He comes again. Belief in the importance of the church is a vital and fundamental doctrine of Christianity.

It is in the assembling of ourselves together in the local and worldwide church that we experience the "communion of saints." The church is a community where we fellowship together, share in each other's burdens, promise to pray for one another, and provide practical and spiritual help to those of the body who are in need. During the pandemic of 2020, it was this aspect of our community that we missed the most. As a church community, we are a body with many parts, gifts, and functions "in whom the whole structure, being joined together, grows into a holy temple in the Lord" (Eph. 2:21).

Jesus only has one plan, and it is called "church." At Caesarea Philippi, He informed His disciples in clear terms of His intentions: "I will build my church, and the gates of hell shall not prevail against it" (Matt. 16:18). The church is not plan B, an afterthought following the failure of Israel, as some continue to teach. For whatever reason—post-Enlightenment individualism or a feeling that the church is too sterile and true Christianity needs to break free of forms and institutions—the church has too often been viewed as secondary and unimportant in our time. The creed corrects that point of view and underscores the church's central importance.

Gospel Forgiveness

Sixth, the creed draws attention to the gospel. "I believe . . . in the forgiveness of sins." Sin is our most basic problem. By nature, we are not right with God. We need forgiveness. This cannot be brought about simply by divine fiat. Forgiveness is a serious business involving the holiness of God and the integrity of His law. It requires the substitutionary, penal death of Jesus—the sufferings of hell as the creed has just spelled out—to remove its stain and guilt from our account. Grace and grace *alone* can rid our souls of the blight of sin. Grace represents the possibility of forgiveness for a wounded, troubled conscience. It means that we stand complete in Christ.

A man distressed about sin wrote to Martin Luther. The Reformer, who himself had suffered long agonies over this problem, replied: "Learn to know Christ and him crucified. Learn to sing to him and say—Lord Jesus, you are my righteousness, I am your sin. You took on you what was mine; you set on me what was yours. You became what you were not that I might become what I was not."[8]

John Bunyan describes the experience in *The Pilgrim's Progress:*

Now I saw in my dream, that the highway up which Christian was to go, was fenced on either side with a wall, and that wall was called Salvation (Isa. 26:1). Up this way, therefore, did burdened Christian run, but not without great difficulty, because of the load on his back. He ran thus till he came at a place somewhat ascending; and upon that place stood a cross, and a little below, in the bottom, a sepulchre. So I saw in my dream, that just as Christian came up with the cross, his burden loosed from off his shoulders, and fell from off his back, and began to tumble, and so continued to do till it came to the mouth of the sepulchre, where it fell in, and I saw it no more.[9]

Nor should we think of this forgiveness as a onetime experience at the inception of our coming to faith in Christ. It is a daily experience this side of eternity. Every single day we sin in thought, word, and deed, and we need to experience afresh the cleansing blood of

Christ and peace of conscience that follows. In the *daily* prayer Jesus gave us, we are to ask, "Forgive us our debts."

Seventh, the Apostles' Creed affirms *our Christian hope.* "I believe in the resurrection of the body and the life everlasting." This world, for its God-given beauty and opportunity, is not our home. We are destined for a life in a new heavens and new earth with a brand-new body. As Paul makes clear, that body will not be identical to our present one (1 Cor. 15:35–49). What is reaped is not what is sown. A seed is sown, it dies, and it comes to life and grows. So it will be with our resurrection bodies. "What you sow is not the body that is to be" (v. 37).

One thing is certain: our resurrected bodies will be glorious. As I wrote elsewhere:

> The Scriptures provide us with some clues as to what this glory might be.
>
> The first is the transfiguration of Christ. On the mountain, Peter saw Christ receiving glory from God (2 Pet. 1:17). John beheld his glory as of the only Son from the Father (Jn. 1:14). There is a weight to the glory of Christ. The transfiguration was not a divinization of Jesus' body. But it was a glimpse of what the body of Jesus could become when freed from the weakness of this world. *Our* resurrection bodies will similarly bear a weightiness and significance, suited for the experience of seeing Christ "face to face" (1 Cor. 13:12).[10]

I believe . . . do you?

Music: Psalms, Hymns, and Spiritual Songs

And do not get drunk with wine, for that is debauchery, but be filled with the Spirit, addressing one another in psalms and hymns and spiritual songs, singing and making melody to the Lord with your heart, giving thanks always and for everything to God the Father in the name of our Lord Jesus Christ, submitting to one another out of reverence for Christ. (Eph. 5:18–21)

Let the word of Christ dwell in you richly, teaching and admonishing one another in all wisdom, singing psalms and hymns and spiritual songs, with thankfulness in your hearts to God. (Col. 3:16)[1]

In a letter to Emperor Trajan, the first-century Roman author and natural philosopher Pliny comments about "Christians" meeting on the Lord's Day and singing the psalms. Similarly, toward the close of the second century, the North African theologian Tertullian writes about Christians singing the Scriptures from the heart to each other when they gather together.

When Christians worship, they sing. In the setting of our current "worship wars," it is tempting to think that Paul was anticipating a rapprochement between classical and contemporary forms of worship and includes, along with psalms and hymns, "spiritual songs" (aka "contemporary" songs). This is hardly what Paul had in mind. What do these three categories mean?

The term "psalms" refers to the Old Testament book of Psalms, while the other two terms have little by way of distinction. "Hymns" refers to the growing set of songs about Christ in the New Testament (Luke 1:46–55, 68–79; 2:29–32; Phil. 2:6–11; Col. 1:15–20). And "spiritual songs" [2] may mean "songs from the Spirit," suggesting some kind of spontaneous, free-flowing singing inspired by the Holy Spirit.[3] Whatever they were, they did not survive for us to examine.

What has survived is a group of around forty songs/poems called *The Odes of Solomon* coming from the close of the first century. They are in Syriac and represent the Oriental or Eastern side of the developing church. In Hughes Oliphant Old's view, they are similar to the canticles in Luke's gospel and are full of evangelical fervor.[4]

Nor should the hymns and spiritual songs be viewed as effectively "taking over" from the psalms, replacing the psalms in favor of a wholly new covenant expression of praise. Hughes Old comments, "It seems much more likely that the earliest Christians understood their hymnody as a sort of elaboration, a sort of drawing out, a commentary, or perhaps a sort of meditation on the canonical psalms and canticles traditionally used in the worship of the Temple and the synagogue."[5]

Both of these passages, in Ephesians and Colossians, reflect the use of songs in worship for the purposes of teaching (instructional and positive) and admonition (warning and negative). Both words are used earlier in Colossians to describe the nature of Paul's preaching and teaching ministry (Col. 1:28), and as Douglas Moo observes, "'teaching' refers to the positive presentation of the truth, while 'admonishing' refers to the more negative warning about the danger of straying from the truth."[6]

Singing "psalms and hymns and spiritual songs" is a way for members of the church to teach and admonish one another. There is, therefore, a horizontal as well as a vertical dimension to the use of songs in worship. Not only is singing songs a way of expressing our love and devotion to the Lord; it is also a way of engaging in the "communion of saints"—the shared responsibility we have for each other's growth and development as believers. This is something the church worldwide was not able to do in any meaningful fashion during the pandemic of 2020 when Christians largely gathered in the confines of their own homes.

Community singing is a vital aspect of corporate worship. I vividly recall bringing an unchurched teenager (from the United Kingdom) to an evening service and afterward asking him what he thought about it. Fully expecting him to make some comment about the sermon, what took him by surprise was the fervency of the singing. The only comparison he could make was the way people sang at professional soccer games. "They sang as though they believed what they sang," he quipped. Would that this was always so!

Music

The New Testament provides us with ample grounds for the inclusion of music in the worship of God. In addition to the identical commands in Ephesians and Colossians, there are the following examples:

- Paul and Silas in prison in Philippi, their feet fastened to stocks, are singing hymns to God at midnight (Acts 16:25).

- Correcting the abuse of *glossolalia* (speaking in an unknown tongue), Paul insists that worship, including what is sung, be understood: "I will sing praise with my spirit, but I will sing with my mind also" (1 Cor. 14:15).

- James exhorts Christians who find themselves in a cheerful spirit to sing praise to God (James 5:13).

Furthermore, there are a number of identifiable lyrics such as the *Amen, Alleluia,* and the *Trisagion—Holy, holy, holy,* which demonstrate a received liturgical tradition in the New Testament church. And no one reading the book of Revelation can fail to note that the church triumphant in heaven is constantly singing (e.g., Rev. 5:9; 14:3; 15:3). And there are what appear to be "songs" or "canticles" in Luke's gospel that some scholars believe to be catechetical material set to music and sung for the purposes of instruction and worship:[7]

- Mary's *Magnificat*[8] (1:46–55)
- Zechariah's *Benedictus*[9] (1:68–79)
- The angelic *Gloria in Excelsis Deo*[10] (2:14)
- Simeon's *Nunc Dimittis*[11] (2:29–32)

Furthermore, as we have alluded to in a previous chapter, there is ample evidence in the New Testament of what appear to be hymn-like texts that perhaps predate the New Testament books and were composed during the generation after the death and resurrection of

Christ. Examples of such pre-New Testament "hymns" are the elaborate praise for Christ in Philippians, Colossians, and John:

> [Have this mind among yourselves, which is yours in Christ
> Jesus],
> who, though he was in the form of God,
> did not count equality with God a thing to be grasped,
> but emptied himself, by taking the form of a servant,
> being born in the likeness of men.
> And being found in human form,
> he humbled himself by becoming obedient to the point of death,
> even death on a cross.

> Therefore God has highly exalted him
> and bestowed on him the name that is above every name,
> so that at the name of Jesus every knee should bow,
> in heaven and on earth and under the earth,
> and every tongue confess that Jesus Christ is Lord,
> to the glory of God the Father. (Phil. 2:5–11)

And,

> He is the image of the invisible God, the firstborn of all creation.
> For by him all things were created, in heaven and on earth, visible
> and invisible,
> whether thrones or dominions or rulers or authorities—all things
> were created through him and for him.
> And he is before all things, and in him all things hold together.
> And he is the head of the body, the church.

He is the beginning, the firstborn from the dead, that in everything
    he might be preeminent.
For in him all the fullness of God was pleased to dwell,
and through him to reconcile to himself all things, whether on
    earth or in heaven, making peace by the blood of his cross.
    (Col. 1:15–20)

And perhaps,

And the Word became flesh and dwelt among us,
and we have seen his glory,
glory as of the only Son from the Father,
full of grace and truth. (John 1:14)

The New Testament church, of course, was following the
practice of the Old Testament church. Tracing the roots of New Testament worship into the Old Testament is a massive undertaking,
and here we must summarize the evidence. Chief witness is the book
of Psalms—a collection of "songs" spanning a thousand years.[12]

If we think of temple worship, for example, "hymns of praise"
were sung on entering the temple (Pss. 15; 24) and at the time of sacrifice (Pss. 25–26).[13] The collection of psalms known as the Psalms
of Ascents (Pss. 120–134) is thought to have been compiled after
the exile and used by pilgrims making their way to celebrate Passover
and other stated calendrical feasts in the restored Jerusalem temple.
In the worship of the second temple, specific psalms were employed
on different days of the week, starting with Sunday—Psalms 24, 48,
82, 94, 81, 93, and 92 for the Sabbath.

In exile, with no temple to worship in, the faithful worshiped in the synagogue and were unable to offer sacrifices. Synagogue worship majored on teaching the Torah and prayer. But significantly, the synagogue liturgy employed the singing of psalms, though without the elaborate instrumental accompaniment that was a part of temple worship. Psalm 137 gives us a vivid description of exiles in Babylon in worship, as Old suggests, with "heavy hearts":[14]

> By the waters of Babylon,
>   there we sat down and wept,
>   when we remembered Zion.
> On the willows there
>   we hung up our lyres.
> For there our captors
>   required of us songs,
>   and our tormentors, mirth, saying,
>   "Sing us one of the songs of Zion!" (Ps. 137:1–3)

The singing of psalms remained part of the tradition of church worship throughout the two millennia since the emergence of the New Testament church. At the Reformation, the Reformed churches continued the practice of singing psalms. The difference, of course, was that they were now sung in the "common tongue" (as opposed to Latin) and by the entire congregation (as opposed to choirs only).

Not all churches are happy about singing material other than the psalms or about the inclusion of instrumental accompaniment. In the denomination to which I belong (Associate Reformed Presbyterian Church), the "Reformed" part of the name is a reference to our ecclesiastical cousins (now called the Reformed Presbyterian Church of North America) who continue to practice *exclusive unaccompanied* psalm singing in their worship services. But is this practice justifiable?

To exclude instrumental accompaniment implies that these instruments functioned in a *ceremonial* fashion only and ceased along with other Levitical ceremonies when Christ appeared and fulfilled the ceremonial meaning of these typological rituals. Like the sacrifices, musical instruments in some way are to be viewed as some kind of prefigurement of Christ, and once He appeared, there is no further need for instrumental or choral accompaniment. There is little logic to the argument.

One major difficulty with exclusive psalm singing is the fact we never actually sing the name of Jesus. The psalms may *allude* to Christ, but they never once mention Him *by name*. It seems strange logic to say that we can pray the name of Christ and read the name of Christ and preach the name of Christ *but not sing His name*! Again, the logic seems astray.

The Reformation

Differences over the exact use of songs and musical accompaniment existed between Luther and Calvin and the traditions that followed them. Luther loved music and was himself an accomplished musician. He encouraged choirs and the use of polyphony. Luther's hymns were characterized by "a plain melody, a strong harmony and a stately rhythm."[15] Calvin had the cathedral organ in Geneva locked and viewed hymns as "man-made" and preferred *a cappella* or unaccompanied singing. Despite this, the hymn "I Greet Thee Who My Sure Redeemer Art" is usually ascribed to Calvin. Also, his worship service included the singing of other scriptural materials.

While I disagree with the insistence upon exclusive psalm singing, it seems clear that the church ought to proceed with *inclusive* psalm singing. Several reasons may be given to justify the singing of Old Testament psalms in New Testament churches:

- The gospel operates in precisely the same way in both testaments. We may sing the psalms with the additional light of the new covenant to add even greater significance to what they say. To cite Augustine, there are matters in the psalms that are latent, matters that are made patent in the new.
- The psalms were the church's songbook until the eighteenth century.
- What do Christians sing when they are unhappy? The answer: the songs of lament and imprecation in the book of Psalms. There are times when we don't feel like singing. It is at such times that Psalm 137 comes into its own. Speaking as it does of days in Babylonian captivity when they hung their harps on willow branches, it vividly depicts days when the joy has been taken from us. A diet of "I am H_A_P_P_Y" songs would be both insincere and naive in such circumstances.

Style

Too often, stylistic matters are relegated to a matter of personal choice as though style has no virtue of its own. That is a naive position to hold. Good-better-best applies to music and musical accompaniment as much as it does to any other art form. But allow me to make some practical suggestions as to music:

- Note the exhortation in Colossians and Ephesians to teach and admonish each other. Do we sing to the Lord? Yes, but we are also exhorting each other. If we see worship as quiet meditation (the worship traditions that emphasize silence and inner meditation), then it can quickly become very individualistic. Worship quickly becomes something about me and God. But if the nature of worship—gathered worship on the Lord's Day—is collective, about the body of Christ as a whole, then singing is an ideal form to get into each other's space. It is difficult to make it about me when I have to listen to others singing and I have to join in. Singing is a way of exhorting each other and teaching each other.

- There is something about the level of intensity with which we sing. We are to be "filled with the Spirit" (the contrast is being drunk with wine), suggesting that the loss of inhibition may have something to do with it. Don't be shy. Sing! "But I can't sing!" you may reply. "Sing anyway," would be my response. Sing "with/in your heart," suggesting sincerity, affection, commitment, and genuineness.

- A word about hymn choice. We have favorites and hymns we dislike. Some of it is sheer prejudice. Generally speaking, churches are poorly educated about music. There are issues of snobbery. For my part, we should try to sing a good variety of hymns and not repeat them too often. In our church, we keep very close track of what is sung and when it is sung. The opening hymn should be about the worship of our triune God. The hymn before the reading of Scripture and the sermon often reflects the theme of the Holy Spirit's work in illuminating Scripture and empowering the preaching. And the closing hymn often reflects the central message of the sermon, calling us to action and commitment.

- And, as we noted in a previous chapter, there is a fascinating moment in Hebrews 2 when the author cites from Psalm 22 a description of Jesus' singing along with the church: "I will tell of your name to my brothers; in the midst of the congregation I will sing your praise" (Heb. 2:12; Ps. 22:22).

It is such a marvelous picture, suggesting that as we sing in worship, Jesus is right at our shoulders, singing along with us and taking such joy in calling us "brothers and sisters." Surely, that is an incentive to sing and make melody in our hearts.

10

Baptism

B aptism is central to the church's mission.[1] Jesus said so. "All authority in heaven and on earth has been given to me. Go therefore and make disciples of all nations, baptizing them in the name of the Father and of the Son and of the Holy Spirit, teaching them to observe all that I have commanded you. And behold, I am with you always, to the end of the age" (Matt. 28:18–20). Jesus charged the fledgling church to

- make disciples from around the globe;
- baptize disciples in the name of the Father, Son, and Holy Spirit; and
- teach disciples everything Jesus had taught them.

The New Testament does not envisage unbaptized Christians except in cases such as that of the dying thief for whom no opportunity to be baptized exists. Baptism is not necessary for salvation, but it is necessary for discipleship.

Baptism is essential, but who are its subjects? On this issue, a fundamental disagreement exists among Christians. Put simply, why do some churches (including Presbyterians, Methodists, and Episcopalians) baptize infants, and some (Baptists) do not? What is the rationale for *paedo*baptism?

Curiously, given the dominical mandate of the Great Commission in Matthew 28, no specific text exists stating that infants—specifically, infants with at least one believing parent—are to be baptized. That silence is sufficient for some to conclude that infants should not receive baptism. But there is no specific text in Scripture that warrants women's receiving the Lord's Supper or that outlines the doctrine of the Trinity in the orthodox manner of the Nicene Creed. These are logical and necessary inferences drawn from Scripture by "good and necessary consequence."[2] From one perspective, silence can mean that something is so obvious it does not need a specific mention.

Before we can address the issue of the baptism of infants, we need to ask a more fundamental question: What is the meaning of baptism?

The Meaning of Baptism

Baptism in one sense is a *washing*, in just the same way that the Lord's Supper is a *meal*. Frequently, in a credobaptist[3] understanding, baptism is viewed as a sign of the faith of the one baptized. If this is the meaning of baptism, it cannot therefore apply to infants who are incapable of expressing faith. In this instance, the very definition of baptism proves the invalidity of paedobaptism.

Clearly, therefore, if a path to paedobaptism is to be found, a *different* answer must be given as to the meaning of baptism. Take, for example, the path of the Westminster Confession of Faith on the meaning of baptism:

> Baptism is a sacrament of the New Testament . . . a sign and seal of the covenant of grace.[4]

And what exactly is a sacrament?

> Sacraments are holy signs and seals of the covenant of grace.[5]

Putting aside the issue of the use of the Latin term *sacramentum* and whether this actually helps us understand baptism (or the Lord's Supper) better (in my opinion it does not), the point here is that the meaning of baptism lies outside any personal response on the part of the candidate for baptism. Specifically, the Westminster Confession's approach underlines a number of important details:

First, the use of the term "signs and seals" is taken directly from Paul's use of it in Romans when he is addressing the Old Testament sacrament of circumcision: "He received the sign of circumcision as a seal of the righteousness that he had by faith while he was still uncircumcised" (Rom. 4:11). Baptism functions in exactly the same way that circumcision functioned in the Abrahamic covenant. That some link exists between the meaning of circumcision and baptism is evidenced by the way Paul switches from one to the other in Colossians 2:11–12: "In him also you were circumcised with a circumcision made without hands, by putting off the body of the flesh, by the circumcision of Christ, having been buried with him in baptism, in which you were also raised with him through faith in the powerful working of God, who raised him from the dead." Note that since circumcision was applied to male infants at the age of eight days, it clearly did not function as a sign of the infant's faith.

Second, consider what signs do. A sign on the side of a road that says "London 186 miles" is saying nothing about the sign itself (e.g., "I am made of metal"); rather, it is stating an objective fact that London exists 186 miles from this spot. Analogously, baptism is a sign *to* faith of forgiveness, the removal of sin and its consequences, justification, adoption, sanctification, glorification. To the one who believes, these things are true. It is not a sign *of* faith but a sign *to* faith.

Nor is it a sign of the inherent power of baptism to accomplish these blessings automatically by what is referred to as "baptismal regeneration." The application of water does not say anything at all about the condition of the heart at the time of baptism or immediately afterward. There is nothing magical about the water. Indeed, even though the water is "set apart as holy" and "useful" (to cite the language of 2 Tim. 2:20–23), I often pour some water on the ground before a baptism simply to underline that it is "just water."[6]

Third, a *seal* functions as a corroborative assurance to the one who is baptized of the truthfulness of the sign. Specifically, the truthfulness and trustworthiness of the "covenant of grace," God's word of promise and assurance that in Christ there is total and complete forgiveness of sin, union and communion with God, and the hope of glory to come.

The Mode of Baptism

For some, the language of baptism, for example, in a passage like Romans 6, proves that the only valid mode of baptism is immersion: "We were buried therefore with him by baptism into death, in order that, just as Christ was raised from the dead by the glory of the Father, we too might walk in newness of life" (v. 4).

The movement is first downward and then upward, into the water and then out of it again. Similarly, the references in the Gospels to those who were baptized by John the Baptist "in the river Jordan" (Matt. 3:6) suggest to some immersion under the Jordan waters despite the fact that it is also equally feasible for the waters to have been shallow and that they stood in the river as John poured water over their heads.

Similarly, in the account of the conversion of the Ethiopian eunuch, when Philip and the eunuch came across some water, Philip stopped the chariot and baptized him. Luke's description includes the words "and they both went down into the water.... And ... they came up out of the water" (Acts 8:38–39). Going down into and coming up out of might suggest immersion, but it could equally be understood otherwise. It may simply have been standing water, and they stood ankle deep in it. We simply do not know. Indeed, we are not specifically told what the mode of baptism was in the New Testament. Again, the silence of the New Testament on this issue requires a more nuanced approach.

One pertinent fact is the way baptism is used in relation to the Holy Spirit. In the forty days after His resurrection, Jesus appeared to the disciples, teaching them further about the kingdom of God. Luke records Jesus saying to them, "John baptized with water, but you will be baptized with the Holy Spirit not many days from now" (Acts 1:5). The reference is to Pentecost and the giving of the Spirit in fuller measure. When Pentecost arrived and "they were all filled with the Holy Spirit" (Acts 2:4), Peter drew attention to the prophecy of Joel: "And in the last days it shall be, God declares, that I will pour out my Spirit on all flesh" (Acts 2:17; cf. Joel 2:28–32).

The mode by which they were baptized with the Holy Spirit is specifically referred to as *pouring*. It seems more than reasonable to conclude that the connection Jesus drew between John's baptism and Pentecost should also include a harmony as to the mode of baptism. The issue may not at first appear to have very much significance.

Surely, we can agree to differ on this point. But the matter becomes a little more difficult if we insist that the only correct mode of baptism is immersion. Are we therefore to immerse infants?[7] Surely not!

It is fascinating to consider how Paul and Peter employ the term *baptism*. Both employ the term in a context when God is initiating a new covenant administration. Paul's use appears in 1 Corinthians 10:1–4, where he speaks of Moses' leading the people through the Red Sea: "All were baptized into Moses in the cloud and in the sea" (v. 2). It is hardly conceivable that we are to think of this as signaling immersion, since Moses and the people walked on dry land.

Similarly, when Peter employs the term, it is in a notoriously difficult section when Peter brings up the time when God established a covenant with Noah. Having mentioned the preparation of an ark and that "eight persons" were "brought safely through water," Peter adds, "Baptism, which corresponds to this, now saves you, not as a removal of dirt from the body but as an appeal to God for a good conscience, through the resurrection of Jesus Christ" (1 Peter 3:20–21). Again, the eight persons on the ark who experienced this water ordeal were not in the water but above it. The symbolism in both passages points away from immersion.

The Subjects of Baptism

The New Testament, as we have seen, clearly advocates that *believers* ought to be baptized. Those who make a credible profession of faith in Jesus Christ, and who have not been baptized as children, ought to receive baptism. In an increasingly secular society, believer's baptism is more frequent even in churches that practice paedobaptism. Typically, they will receive baptism at the time they officially become members of a local church.

In addition, paedobaptists also insist that the children of believing parents ought to receive baptism.[8] This conclusion is arrived at intuitively rather than simply textually. Individual texts and the silence of the New Testament may lead Christians to exact opposite conclusions. However, if we approach the data in a different way, with a different perspective, the data will suggest a certain conclusion.

Several key points need to be made to substantiate the inclusion of infants within God's administration of the new covenant.

First, and the most basic, is the way the New Testament views the church as an organic unity. Stephen, shortly before his death, speaks of the Old Testament era as the "congregation in the wilderness" (Acts 7:38). The word translated "congregation" is, in fact, the basic Greek word for "church" (*ekklēsia*). Surely, therefore, we should expect the administration of New Testament signs and seals to follow a principle of continuity.

Take, for example, the way Paul employs the terms "sign" and "seal" in Romans 4:11 when addressing the issue of circumcision—the sign and seal of the covenant God made with Abraham (Gen. 17:11). As Sinclair Ferguson notes: "Foundational to a biblical theology of baptism is the recognition that baptism's sign character positions it within an ongoing pattern of divine activity. Throughout the history of redemption, God's dealings with his people have always included the use of emblems. His epochal promises were illustrated and confirmed physically as well as verbally."[9] It is therefore fascinating to explore the unfolding covenants and note that each one includes children.

- The covenant with Adam included the Tree of Life as a sacramental symbol and had implication for his offspring (Gen. 2:9; Rom. 5:12–21).

- The covenant with Noah was accompanied by a rainbow and included Noah, his wife, and their three sons and their wives (Gen. 6:18; 8:18; 9:8).
- The covenant with Abraham was accompanied by the ritual of circumcision for eight-day-old boys (Gen. 15:18; 17:1–4, 11).
- The covenant with Moses was signaled by the Sabbath, which included implications for "little ones" (Deut. 29:9–14).
- The covenant with David (2 Sam. 7:8–16) was signaled by David's throne (Ps. 89:3–4) and also had implications for David's offspring (v. 4).

Surely, it is not unwarranted to expect that this "you and your seed" pattern continues in the new covenant. Indeed, what might the expectation of Peter's audience on the day of Pentecost have been when they heard him announce the arrival of the new covenant with its twin emblems of baptism and the Lord's Supper? They were Jews, with built-in expectations that God deals with families as much as He does with individuals. What else would they have understood when Peter said, "The promise is for you and for your children," other than a principle of *continuity* (Acts 2:39)? Had Peter intended to suggest a *discontinuity* of administration, no longer a principle of "you and your seed," he would effectively have excommunicated children from God's redemptive purpose. Surely, as ingrained as this principle was in Jewish minds, Peter would have had to say so clearly and precisely. The fact that he did not say any such thing is surely demonstrating the opposite: that New Testament believers *and their children* are included in the terms of the covenant.

Second is to note precisely what Jesus said regarding infants and the kingdom of God. Despite strong denials by Baptists, the passage where Jesus "blesses" the little children supports the idea of *inclusion*: "And they were bringing children to him that he might touch them, and the disciples rebuked them. But when Jesus saw it, he was indignant and said to them, 'Let the children come to me; do not hinder them, for to such belongs the kingdom of God. Truly, I say to you, whoever does not receive the kingdom of God like a child shall not enter it.' And he took them in his arms and blessed them, laying his hands on them" (Mark 10:13–16; cf. Luke 18:15–17).

Anyone who suggests that Jesus was merely comparing disciples to little children, specifically in terms of qualities such as meekness and humility, clearly has not spent much time with children! On the contrary, Jesus is pointing out a class of kingdom members—"for to such" (Greek *toioutos*). The kingdom of God includes children. Moreover, the word Luke employs is even more specific (Greek *brephos*) and refers to nursing infants. In other words, the kingdom of God is made up of mothers who are coming to Jesus (implying they believed in Him) together with their infant children. Nor should we think of Jesus as blessing the children in some sentimental fashion.

Blessing is a profoundly covenantal term, employed in the so-called Aaronic benediction of Numbers 6:

"The LORD bless you and keep you;
the LORD make his face to shine upon you and be gracious to you;
the LORD lift up his countenance upon you and give you peace."
(Num. 6:24–26)

Third, the use of the term "house" or "household" when baptism occurred again signals the inclusion of infants. True, this is an argument from silence, but the pressure of sacramental administrative continuity suggests that a family principle is operative (e.g., Acts 10:2; 16:15, 33–34; 18:8; 1 Cor. 1:16). The Greek word for "house" (*oikos*) translates a Hebrew word that throughout the Old Testament signifies the entire family.[10] The inclusion of infants in God's covenantal dealings is reinforced by the way that the New Testament addresses children. As Sinclair Ferguson notes: "This continuity is further exhibited in the way in which Paul's letters include children as 'saints' and exhort them to fulfill specifically covenantal responsibilities: 'Obey your parents *in the Lord* for this is right' (Eph. 1:1; 6:1–3; cf. Col. 1:2; 3:20). Paul's appeal to the Mosaic covenant in the Ephesians context implies that the same covenant dynamic which grounded the relationship of parents and children in the old continues in the new."[11]

The Timing of Baptism

How long should parents wait for baptism? Because of health concerns and the advent of child vaccinations, it is now highly unusual to baptize (as I once did in my first charge) a baby in the same week that she was born. Additionally, the difficulty of gathering families together often means that children are already walking before they are baptized. I do not wish to make light of either concern. However, if baptism is the sign and seal of the covenant of grace, infants ought to receive it as soon as is practically possible.

11

The Lord's Supper

In the previous chapter, we looked at the initiatory covenant sign of baptism. In this chapter, we will briefly examine the confirmatory covenant sign of the Lord's Supper.[1] As with baptism, the church has been and remains divided on almost all aspects of the sacrament, resulting in considerable differences of opinion both within and between various denominations. We cannot possibly cover all these issues in this chapter, but we will single out some of the more important matters.

What Is the Meaning of the Lord's Supper?

Matthew and Mark give almost identical accounts of the initiation of the supper by Jesus in the upper room. Jesus took some bread, broke it, distributed it to the disciples, and said, "Take, eat; this is my body." Then the cup: "Drink of it, all of you, for this is my blood of the covenant, which is poured out for many for the forgiveness of sins" (Matt. 26:26–28; see Mark 14:22–25). Luke adds the words "Do this in remembrance of me" (Luke 22:19–20). And Paul cites these words too (1 Cor. 11:24–25; Paul and Luke spent a lot of time together). These slight variations are due to the fact that the original words would have been in Aramaic, and different oral traditions occurred in translation.

As we begin to think of the precise meaning of the Lord's Supper, several important clues arise.

First, *the Lord's Supper is a covenantal meal replacing Passover.*[2] The meal was instituted by Jesus at the time of Passover. Several important Old Testament allusions are clearly mentioned:

- "Blood of the covenant" recalls its use in Exodus 24:8 at the time of the ratification of the Mosaic covenant. How fitting, then, since the Mosaic covenant is now regarded as "the ministry of death" and "condemnation" (2 Cor. 3:7–9), that the inauguration of the new covenant signs and seals should point to the "once for all" shedding of Christ's blood as substitute and satisfaction for sin (Rom. 6:10; Heb. 7:27; 9:12, 26; 10:10).

- The otherwise curious phrase "for many" makes perfect sense when we recall that this is an allusion to the final words of the fourth Servant Song in Isaiah: "Yet he bore the sin of many" (Isa. 53:12). This is not the only occasion that Jesus refers to this Servant Song. In what appears to be something of a "mission statement" regarding His purpose in the world, Jesus said, "For even the Son of Man came not to be served but to serve, and to give his life as a ransom *for many*" (Mark 10:45, emphasis added). It is not unreasonable to think that from childhood, Jesus memorized these songs because they spoke so clearly to His purpose.

- The reference to the "new covenant" recalls Jeremiah's promise: "Behold, the days are coming, declares the LORD, when I will make a new covenant with the house of Israel and the house of Judah" (Jer. 31:31). And, as the author of Hebrews makes clear, "In speaking of a new covenant, he makes the first one obsolete. And what is becoming obsolete and growing old is ready to vanish away" (Heb. 8:13). Again, how fitting that on the night of Passover, Jesus should announce the dawning of the new covenant era at this moment—the week of His death and resurrection. The old covenant is gone; an upgrade is launched—an unbreakable bond with promises and expectations.

Like Passover, the Lord's Supper is a family meal. God's children celebrate it in anticipation of the "marriage supper of the Lamb" (Rev. 19:9) in the new heavens and earth.

Second, *the Lord's Supper is a sensory experience of union with Christ.* The term "communion" (Greek *koinonia*) is elsewhere translated "fellowship" or "participation" in the New Testament. For example: "The cup of blessing that we bless, is it not a participation in the blood of Christ? The bread that we break, is it not a participation in the body of Christ?" (1 Cor. 10:16). Paul's point in this passage in 1 Corinthians is to argue for the closest possible bond between the sign (bread, wine) and that which the sign signifies (Christ's body and blood). There is a fellowship, a participation, that occurs at the supper with Christ's human nature, His body and blood. The question is, What kind of fellowship? What kind of participation? In brief, what does the word "is" mean in "This *is* my body," "This *is* my blood"? Here, the church has been divided.

The issues are complex, and we can only summarize the issues here. Some have argued that the fellowship is nothing more than a "remembering." After all, did not Jesus say, "Do this in remembrance of me" (Luke 22:19)? Focusing on the word "remembrance" draws attention to the fact that the supper is an act of recollection. Just as when we look at a photograph of a deceased friend or loved one, we recall conversations and events stored up in our memory. The supper functions, then, as a trigger. We remember Jesus' words written in Scripture, and we are comforted and blessed as we do so. That this is an aspect of the supper cannot be denied. And large sections of conservative churches, particularly in Britain, hold to a "memorialist" view of the supper. But is this all there is to the supper? Does the term "participate" (communion, fellowship) mean something more?

Others have gone further, a great deal further, and suggest (with varying degrees) that something actually happens to the bread and wine. At its most intense, Roman Catholics and some Episcopalians believe that once the bread and wine are consecrated, they become Christ's flesh and blood. Whatever the average Roman Catholic may think when eating the bread or drinking the wine (and at various times in church history, participants were not always given both bread *and* wine), Roman Catholic scholars did not intend for this change to be a literal one. Employing a sophisticated Aristotelian distinction between "form" and "accident," Roman Catholic theologians intended that a "thing" may look (and, more importantly, taste) like bread and wine, but in another dimension/reality, it is something very different, in this case the body and blood of Christ. In a less precise way, Lutherans argued that Jesus' body and blood is "in" or "with" or "under" the bread and wine, though it is difficult to understand the precise nature of the union.

In order to analyze the Roman Catholic (*transubstantiation*) and Lutheran (*consubstantiation*) views, a specific question needs to be addressed: Where is the body of Jesus right now? Note that we are asking a question as to His *human* nature, not His *divine* nature. As to the latter, it is everywhere. The divine nature of Jesus is, to use the technical term, *ubiquitous*. There is not a square inch of the entire universe where the divine nature of Jesus is not found. As we participate in the supper, we commune with Jesus, who (according to His divine nature) is everywhere present. However, the supper draws attention not to His divine nature but to His human nature. Our fellowship is with His *body* and *blood*. But where are they? The simplest answer is "in heaven." When Jesus passed through the veil that separates this world from the realm where departed saints and angelic beings exist, He took His physical body with Him. It remains a physical body. It will forever remain so. And, crucial to the issue at hand, the human nature of Jesus does not possess the property of ubiquity. His flesh and blood can only occupy one part of the universe at a time. The suggestion that His flesh and blood can come into our world in multiple locations at the same time is not simply an error in our understanding of the supper; it is an error, and a very basic one at that, in Christology. This, in part, was Calvin's response to Lutheranism.

But we have yet to answer the question as to the nature of the participation that believers enjoy in the supper. How, precisely, do we commune with Christ's body and blood at the table? Calvin's magisterial answer to this question was "by the secret power of the Holy Spirit."[3] The Holy Spirit is able to unite us with the body and blood of Christ, *which remains in heaven*. His body and blood are not only an assurance of our forgiveness and acceptance as His family; they are also a guarantee of our future resurrection. The communion is a spiritual one, a specific work of the Holy Spirit.

Third, the Lord's Supper is *a gospel meal designed for Christians prone to amnesia*. In Paul's words, whenever one partakes of the supper, "you proclaim the Lord's death" (1 Cor. 11:26). The supper preaches. The supper (and for that matter, baptism) is, in Augustine's famous term for the sacraments, "a visible word."[4] The supper speaks of the gospel, God's good word of forgiveness and adoption to sinners who believe in Jesus Christ. We are prone to forget that there is nothing we can *do* to earn God's favor. It is a gift, an "inexpressible gift" (2 Cor. 9:15). In the words of the eighteenth-century hymnwriter Robert Robinson,

> Prone to wander, Lord I feel it,
> Prone to leave the God I love.[5]

We need frequent reminders of the gospel because we are hardwired to self-justification. The supper is designed to act as both sign and seal of gospel privileges.

Who Is the Supper For?

A segment of the church has argued that the Lord's Supper should include infants, in the same manner as baptism.[6] The church's response to this has noted that Passover, a meal of lamb and bitter herbs, was not given to nursing infants, and furthermore, Paul calls on the Corinthians to an act of self-examination and discernment when participating in the supper (1 Cor. 11:28–29). Clearly, these are actions infants cannot perform. Scholars suggest that it was the middle of the third century before infant or *paedo*-communion appeared.[7]

Historic Reformed and Presbyterian churches and confessions have opposed the practice of paedocommunion, insisting that the supper is to be given only to baptized Christians who are members in good standing in a local church. The issue arises because of the potential for participating in the supper "in an unworthy manner" (1 Cor. 11:27). Technically, this is called *manducatio indignorum* (unworthy eating). And it is here that earnest Christians may too easily slip into a form of legalism. If an ability for self-examination and discernment is a perquisite for communion, how much of it is required? This has led in some churches to an overly fastidious "preparation," suggesting that a certain degree of holiness (marks of saving faith) needs to be exhibited before participating in the supper. Add to that a preliminary visitation by the elders and the history of "communion tokens" to be presented at the time of the supper as proof of their "good standing," and an almost inevitable legalism enters, upending the very nature of the gospel the supper intends to convey. Worse, and almost counterintuitively, reluctance to come to the supper on the grounds of an insufficient "sense of sin" could (and did) become a mark of maturity. Indeed, the very fact of not taking the supper could then be seen as a distinctive mark of piety. Only immature believers participate in the supper! The story is often repeated that "Rabbi Duncan" (his name was John Duncan, but he was professor of Oriental languages, and hence the nickname) told a congregant who was reluctant to partake of the supper because of her sin, "Take it, woman; it's for sinners!"

It needs to be remembered that the only account of the observation of the supper we have in the New Testament is in the case of the wholly dysfunctional church in Corinth, a church whose dysfunctionality may not reflect the average church in any way. The "harsh" tone and dire threats Paul issued were pertinent for Corinth but may not necessarily have found expression at Philippi or Ephesus. A practice of "fencing" the table that mimics Paul's pastoral response to Corinth's flagrant sins may unduly deter genuine Christians from participation and turn the supper into an occasion for dread and fear rather than joy and celebration. It is interesting that the church has often chosen to read the words of institution in 1 Corinthians 11 rather than the Synoptic Gospel accounts: "Whoever, therefore, eats the bread or drinks the cup of the Lord in an unworthy manner will be guilty concerning the body and blood of the Lord. Let a person examine himself, then, and so eat of the bread and drink of the cup. For anyone who eats and drinks without discerning the body eats and drinks judgment on himself" (1 Cor. 11:27–29).

But why stop at verse 29? If the contexts are meant to be the same, why not include the next verse: "That is why many of you are weak and ill, and some have died" (v. 30)? Never once have I heard anyone read that verse at the Lord's Table. Perhaps, rather than creating a sense of fear and trepidation, one should instead vary one's liturgical approach, employing Jesus' words to the church at Laodicea: "Behold, I stand at the door and knock. If anyone hears my voice and opens the door, I will come in to him and eat with him, and he with me" (Rev. 3:20).[8] It is vital to convey the truth that the supper is for the unworthy, however advanced in holiness we may be.

How Is the Supper to Be Observed?

In addressing the question of how the supper should be celebrated, we will raise four specific issues.

First, the issue of frequency. For my part, this is not an issue of "first importance" (1 Cor. 15:3). Did the New Testament church celebrate the supper every week? Since we do not have any information in the New Testament on the use of the supper other than in Corinth, we cannot answer that question with any certainty. It is often argued that Calvin's view was that the supper ought to be practiced on a weekly basis. But the issue is more nuanced than it might at first appear. One important fact to remember is that Calvin never practiced weekly communion. Given the degree of weekly pastoral scrutiny (all of Geneva were technically "members" of the churches), weekly communion would have been a practical impossibility. Again, Calvin preached around five hourlong sermons at lunchtime on weekdays and two on Sunday. The ratio of preaching to the supper service would have been 6:1. In most churches today, with little sense of a Sabbath principle, there is typically only one service. If the supper is not to be relegated to a fast-moving addendum at the close of the service, the amount of time for preaching is considerably reduced, a price too high for some of us to accept. At First Presbyterian Church, Columbia, the supper is celebrated once a month (eight in the morning and four in the evening). Since it takes around twenty to twenty-five minutes to do it with any sense of dignity and pacing, that ratio seems to be both practical and wise.

Second, there must be some sense in which the two signs and seals of the new covenant are considered *special*. If, for example, we adopt the view of Calvin noted above, where by the power of the Holy Spirit we commune with the body and blood of Christ in heaven, there may be some truth to Robert Bruce's oft-cited words, "We do not get a better Christ, but we do get Christ *better*."[9] The statement has not always been received well, but if true, it adds to the significance we attach to the supper as a sign and seal of the covenant of grace.

Third, we need to be conscious of four directions at the supper.

- *Backward*: Look at the cross and feel your sins and rejoice in atonement.
- *Upward*: Where Christ's ascended body is right now.
- *Forward*: "For as often as you eat this bread and drink the cup, you proclaim the Lord's death *until he comes*" (1 Cor. 11:26, emphasis added). We are pilgrims, on a journey toward home.
- *Around*: We are a body, with Christ as the Head; a building (stones) with Christ as chief cornerstone (1 Peter 2:5–7).

Fourth, the supper is meant to be *joyful*. The cup (alluding to the third cup of the Passover ritual) is a "cup of blessing" (1 Cor. 10:16). The very term "blessing" with covenantal overtones (cf. Num. 6:24–26) is a reminder that in Christ we are promised "every spiritual blessing in the heavenly places" (Eph. 1:3).

Appendix: Private Communion

The Westminster Confession strictly forbids "private communion": "The Supper is to be distributed "to none who are not then present in the congregation."[10] Most congregations who subscribe the confession today interpret that statement in a manner that permits invalids to receive communion in their homes (or nursing facilities), provided there is a minister and a plurality of ruling elders present.

More pertinently at the time of writing, COVID-19 and the worldwide pandemic has forced the consideration of another caveat. Given the closing down of churches (whether mandated by the state or not), the celebration of the supper became impossible. Even when churches reopened, many in the church family did not return. As I write, less than a third of the members have returned. If, for example, we were to celebrate the supper in person, are we then disenfranchising the rest of the body who are prevented from coming? We have been at pains to underline the genuineness of their participation in worship through virtual means. In the days when only a handful were present in the church, our church members sang with us, read the Scripture with us, prayed with us, and even took sermon notes. I would receive texts and emails and even videos of their participation. We were worshiping *together*, even though in a means the Apostles could never have conceived. But if we celebrate the supper, more than half our church family are cut off from participation. This hardly seems fair.

Leaving aside the sanitary issues involved in having the supper in a pandemic (remember that most churches put aside the use of a single cup a long time ago for individual plastic throwaway cups for similar reasons), the question of the *legitimacy* of at-home communion has arisen. Some hard-hitting blogs have appeared stating the practice to be a violation, emphasizing, among other things, the intent behind the words in Acts 20:7 "when we were *gathered together* to break bread" (emphasis added), leaving aside the issue that these words may refer to a fellowship meal rather than the supper. They gathered in person. *Voila!* But the New Testament does not envisage the situation that the church worldwide is now facing. The question of virtual participation is fraught with practical problems, let alone the issue of whether it is justifiable. Could it be, to employ a distinction Charles Hodge uses when discussing the validity of baptism, that at-home communion, virtually officiated by ministers and elders, be considered irregular but not *invalid*?[11] While every ounce of me wishes I could prove without doubt the necessity of in-person gathering for a valid celebration of the supper, we have already conceded at-home communion as valid for the invalid and deemed all other aspects of virtual worship valid. Whatever the answer, one that cannot be deemed correct is one that demotes the supper as something that the church can live without.

12

The Benediction

I wonder what you think about the benediction at the end of the service. The minister raises his hands, mimicking a practice seen in Aaron and Jesus (Lev. 9:22; Luke 24:50), and (in our church) urges worshipers to keep their eyes open (for reasons we will explain below) and pronounces the words of benediction. Do you, I wonder, think to yourself, "At last! The service is over!" Or do you understand the importance of the words of benediction and the profound encouragement they offer?

Take, for example, the words of the so-called Aaronic benediction:

"The LORD bless you and keep you;
the LORD make his face to shine upon you and be gracious to you;
the LORD lift up his countenance upon you and give you peace."
(Num. 6:24–26)

Or, the benediction that concludes the epistle to the Hebrews:

Now may the God of peace who brought again from the dead our
Lord Jesus, the great shepherd of the sheep, by the blood of the

eternal covenant, equip you with everything good that you may do his will, working in us that which is pleasing in his sight, through Jesus Christ, to whom be glory forever and ever. Amen. (Heb. 13:20–21)

Or, arguably, the most used benediction:

The grace of the Lord Jesus Christ and the love of God and the fellowship of the Holy Spirit be with you all. (2 Cor. 13:14)

Or, the succinct benedictions in 2 Thessalonians, Titus, and Hebrews:

The grace of our Lord Jesus Christ be with you all. (2 Thess. 3:18)

Grace be with you all. (Titus 3:15)

Grace be with all of you. (Heb. 13:25)

These are all examples of benedictions employed in Scripture. But my own use of benedictions was entirely reshaped by the practice of Dale Ralph Davis, who for five sweet years co-labored with me at First Presbyterian Church, Columbia, as the evening preacher. His preaching was rich, expository, engaging, and unique in its delivery. I can think of no one else I would rather listen to on Old Testament historical passages. However, it wasn't merely his preaching that impressed me; it was the manner in which he pronounced the benediction at the close of the service. He not only employed the familiar biblical benedictions cited above (and there are many more, of course); he also composed his own, something that I had never heard done. When he retired in 2018, we presented him with a book containing some of his benedictions.[1] And it has now become my practice to compose benedictions of my own.

A fundamental question arises: Is the benediction a closing liturgical word of blessing, or is it a prayer? If the former, it seems appropriate to keep one's eyes open. If the latter, then it also seems appropriate to close one's eyes. For far too many years, I fell into the view that this was just a kind of Christian "farewell" at the end of the service, at best a prayer (and therefore to be received with heads bowed and eyes closed) rather than its covenantal significance as a blessing (in opposition to a curse) and therefore having very distinctive import theologically, liturgically, and experientially. At the close of the service, Christians are reminded of God's good and kind words of gospel encouragement as they go into the week that lies ahead of them. At every turn, God's covenant mercies will uphold and encourage them as they battle with sin and the devil.

It was Martin Luther who reintroduced into the liturgy of the sixteenth century the pronouncement of a benediction at the close of the service (following its neglect in medieval liturgy). Luther took as his justification the fact that Jesus pronounced a blessing in Bethany, just before the ascension: "Lifting up his hands he blessed them" (Luke 24:50).

It is common, for example, in Presbyterian churches to reserve the Aaronic benediction for the conclusion of a baptism or an ordination of a minister or an office bearer:

"The Lord bless you and keep you;
the Lord make his face to shine upon you and be gracious to you;
the Lord lift up his countenance upon you and give you peace."
(Num. 6:24–26)

Presbyterians have most commonly employed the benediction that concludes Paul's second letter to the Corinthians:

The grace of the Lord Jesus Christ and the love of God and the fellowship of the Holy Spirit be with you all. (2 Cor. 13:14)

Since these words come at the close of a letter that has bristled with controversy and difficulty within this prickly church in Corinth, it has even more significance by way of encouragement.

Here are some more examples from Dale Ralph Davis:

Now a dying Savior's love,
a risen Savior's joy,
an ascended Savior's power,
and returning Savior's hope,
rest upon your hearts and your homes. Amen.

May the companionship of the man of sorrows
and the power of the King of glory
rest upon you this day and all your days. Amen.

The Lord be the shelter above you, the tower around you,
and the rock beneath you all your days until Jesus comes. Amen.

Congregation of the Lord Jesus Christ,
in all your darkness and troubles,
remember what you are and have.
You've been loved with an everlasting love,

you are supported by everlasting arms,
you are the recipients of everlasting life,
and heirs of an everlasting kingdom
all sealed and made sure by the blood of an everlasting Prophet.
Amen.

But what exactly is a *benediction*? What is it meant to do liturgically in the worship service?

Good Word

Literally, the word *benediction* means a "good word." But in what sense is it a *good* word? The answer lies along the recognition that the benediction is also referred to as "the blessing." Think of the Aaronic benediction: "The LORD *bless* you and keep you ..." (Num. 6:24, emphasis added). And blessings (and curses) are associated with God's *covenant*. Simply put, Christians are God's covenant people to whom covenant blessings abound.

Let us remind ourselves of the story of redemption. God builds His church using the scaffolding of successive covenants (a bond with promises to His people). The word *covenant* (Hebrew *berith*, Greek *diathēkē*) first occurs in the story of Noah and his family (Gen. 9:1) and the judgment-flood ordeal (curse, Gen. 6:11–13) from which they were delivered. God made a promise to this family in the form of a *covenant*: "I will establish my covenant with you" (Gen. 6:18). The word "establish" suggests that this was more of a confirmation of an already existing covenant relationship rather than something brand-new. Despite the fact that the term *covenant* does not appear in the description of God's relationship with Adam, the minor prophet

Hosea understood it that way: "But like Adam they transgressed the covenant; there they dealt faithlessly with me" (Hos. 6:7).

As we survey the development of God's story of redemption, we note a pattern of covenants: with Adam, Noah, Abraham, Moses, and the promise of a *new covenant* in the prophecies of Jeremiah and Ezekiel. The promise of God's Deliverer-Seed (Gen. 3:15) would come through Abraham's seed and would bring blessings to the nations (Gen. 12:1–3). When Jesus commissioned the disciples to "make disciples of all nations" (Matt. 28:19), He had the promise-word of the Abrahamic covenant in mind.

A covenant is a voluntary mutual commitment that binds two or more parties together. Covenants may be negotiated (as in a marriage contract), or (as in God's covenants) they may be unilaterally imposed. If the terms of the covenant are violated, curses ensue. As God's children, we are assured that we are in a covenant relationship with Him. The curses that we so rightly deserve have been met in the substitutionary penal death of Christ. His obedience became ours, and our sins became His. In union and communion with Christ, we are blessed—the covenant blessings, *all of them*, are ours. This is the *good word* that is pronounced at the close of the worship service, a reminder of our standing in covenant relationship with God, a reminder of God's sovereign initiative and determination to bring us safely home as well as our commitment and obligation to remain faithful to Him by way of a response to the grace we have received.

Technically, then, to answer the question with which we began this chapter, the benediction is a pronouncement rather than a prayer.[2] And consequently, it is appropriate for the congregation to receive it as God's word of promise to His people.

Gospel Word

Think of it this way. On the first day of the week, we gather together for worship. At the close of the service, we hear God's promissory word of protection and provision, care and counsel, help and hope for the week to come. It is a gospel moment: we are God's adopted children, Jesus is our elder brother, the Holy Spirit is our strengthener and advocate, so come what may, we are safe and secure.

Appendix

Here are some other New Testament benedictions:

Grace to you and peace from God our Father and the Lord Jesus Christ. (Rom. 1:7b)

May the God of hope fill you with all joy and peace in believing, so that by the power of the Holy Spirit you may abound in hope. (Rom. 15:13)

May the God of peace be with you all. Amen. (Rom. 15:33)

Grace to you and peace from God our Father and the Lord Jesus Christ. (1 Cor. 1:3)

Therefore, my beloved brothers, be steadfast, immovable, always abounding in the work of the Lord, knowing that in the Lord your labor is not in vain. (1 Cor. 15:58)

The grace of the Lord Jesus be with you. (1 Cor. 16:23)

Grace to you and peace from God our Father and the Lord Jesus Christ. (2 Cor. 1:2; Gal. 1:3; Eph. 1:2; Phil. 1:2; 2 Thess. 1:2; Philem. 3)

Now to him who is able to do far more abundantly than all that we ask or think, according to the power at work within us, to him be glory in the church and in Christ Jesus throughout all generations, forever and ever. Amen. (Eph. 3:20–21)

Peace be to the brothers, and love with faith, from God the Father and the Lord Jesus Christ. Grace be with all who love our Lord Jesus Christ with love incorruptible. (Eph. 6:23–24)

Grace be with you. (1 Tim. 6:21b)

Grace, mercy, and peace from God the Father and Christ Jesus our Lord. (2 Tim. 1:2b)

Peace to all of you who are in Christ. (1 Peter 5:14b)

Now to him who is able to keep you from stumbling and to present you blameless before the presence of his glory with great joy, to the only God, our Savior, through Jesus Christ our Lord, be glory, majesty, dominion, and authority, before all time and now and forever. Amen. (Jude 24–25)

The grace of the Lord Jesus be with all. Amen. (Rev. 22:21)

And here are a few of my own:

Congregation of the Lord Jesus Christ,
may the waters of life spring up within you to overflowing
so that you may never feel thirsty;

may the waters of life fulfill you in every way
so that your soul will be eternally satisfied in Christ.
In the name of the Father, the Son and the Holy Spirit. Amen.
(Based on John 4)

May the Lord of peace Himself, born in a manger in Bethlehem,
grant you peace at all times, in all circumstances. The Lord be with
you all. Amen. (For Christmas Eve)

May Jesus' promise to build His church and fill her with His glory,
motivate you to labor, rid you of fear, and equip you with power,
until the day dawns and the shadows flee away. Amen.

Now may the God whose affections never waver,
whose love never grows cold,
whose promises never fail,
and whose commitment remains steadfast,
keep you from the evil one,
and from doubt and despair,
until Jesus comes. Amen.

May the Lord, who knows your weakness, make you strong,
may the Lord, who knows your fears, make you unafraid,
may the Lord, who knows your frustrations, make you calm,
in the name of the Father, the Son, and the Holy Spirit. Amen.

Notes

Chapter 1

1   Westminster Confession of Faith, 25:2.

2   Chad Van Dixhoorn, *Confessing the Faith: A Reader's Guide to the Westminster Confession of Faith* (Edinburgh, Scotland: Banner of Truth, 2014), 341.

3   George Barna, *Revolution* (Wheaton, Ill.: Tyndale House, 2005); William P. Young, *The Shack* (Newbury Park, Calif.: Windblown Media, 2007).

4   Brian Sanders, *Life after Church* (Downers Grove, Ill.: InterVarsity Press, 2007); Julia Duin, *Quitting Church* (Grand Rapids, Mich.: Baker, 2008); Wayne Jacobsen and Dave Coleman, *So You Don't Want to Go to Church Anymore* (Los Angeles: Windblown Media, 2006).

5   Theologians have referred to these marks using a variety of labels: *notae, signa, criteria.*

6   Philip Melanchthon, *Loci Communes*, trans. J.A.O. Preus (St. Louis: Concordia, 1992), 137.

7   John Calvin, *Institutes of the Christian Religion*, ed. John T. McNeill, trans. Ford Lewis Battles (Philadelphia: Westminster, 1977), 4.2.3 (2:1045).

8   The Belgic Confession (1561), article 29.

9   John Stott, *Men with a Message* (London: Longmans, 1954), 163–64. Reprinted in the United States as *Basic Introduction to the New Testament* (Grand Rapids, Mich.: Eerdmans, 1964).

10   Mark Dever, *Nine Marks of a Healthy Church* (Wheaton, Ill.: Crossway, 2004).

11   "About Coast Redwoods," California Department of Parks and Recreation, CA.gov, accessed August 7, 2018, https://www.parks.ca.gov/?page_id=22257.

12   John Stott, *Your Mind Matters: The Place of the Mind in the Christian Life* (Downers Grove, Ill.: IVP, 2006).

13   See Eric Wright, *Church—No Spectator Sport: In Search of Spiritual Gifts* (Darlington, England: Evangelical, 2012).

Chapter 2

1   For an in-depth treatment of this issue, see Sinclair Ferguson, *Devoted to God: Blueprints for Sanctification* (Edinburgh, Scotland: Banner of Truth, 2016), 261–71.

2   Cf. Ferguson, *Devoted to God*, 264.

3   See Ferguson, *Devoted to God*, 262; John Murray, *The Epistle to the Romans*, NICNT (Grand Rapids, Mich.: Eerdmans, 1995), 257–59; Peter O'Brien, *Colossians, Philemon*, WBC 44 (Waco, Tex.: Word, 1982), 139.

4   Benjamin B. Warfield, "The Foundations of the Sabbath in the Word of God," in *Selected Shorter Writings of Benjamin B. Warfield*, ed. John E. Meeter, vol. 1, (Phillipsburg, N.J.: Presbyterian and Reformed, 1970), 319.

5   In New England, there were thirty-nine pages of small-print Sabbath laws in the days of the Pilgrims. John Owen once said, "A man can scarcely in six days read over all the duties that are proposed to be observed on the seventh." John Owen, *An Exposition of the Epistle to the Hebrews*, vol. 2, 7 vols. (Edinburgh, Scotland: Banner of Truth, 1991), 441.

6   John Stott, *The Radical Disciple: Wholehearted Christian Living* (Downers Grove, Ill.: IVP, 2010), 59–60.

7   Alexander Whyte, *An Exposition on the Shorter Catechism* (Fearn, Scotland: Christian Focus, 2004), 135.

Chapter 3

1   John Calvin, *The Necessity of Reforming the Church* (repr., Audubon, N.J.: Old Paths, 1994), 7.

2   Chapter 22.1. See my article in *Tabletalk*, "What Is the Regulative Principle?," accessed July 30, 2020, https://www.ligonier.org/blog/what-is-regulative-principle/.

3   "Jenny Geddes," St Giles' Cathedral, accessed March 12, 2021, https://stgilescathedral.org.uk/jenny-geddes/.

4   This section was previously published as Derek W.H. Thomas, "The Regulative Principle of Worship," *Tabletalk* 34 no. 7 (July 2010): 10–13.

5   Augustine, *Tractates on the Gospel of John: 55–111*, trans. John W. Rettig, The Fathers of the Church 90 (Washington, D.C.: Catholic University of America Press, 1994), 117.

6   Matthew Pinson, ed., *Perspectives on Christian Worship: 5 Views* (Nashville, Tenn.: B&H Academic, 2009), 114–15.

Chapter 4

1   Philip Schaff, *History of the Christian Church* (1910; repr., Grand Rapids, Mich.: Kregel, 1994), 1:458–59.

2   Ferguson defines "things indifferent" as those things that "are not specifically, or in detail, mandated by Scripture."

3   Sinclair B. Ferguson, foreword to *Reformation Worship: Liturgies from the Past for the Present*, eds. Jonathan Gibson and Mark Earngey (Greensboro, N.C.: New Growth, 2018), xv–xvi. The Westminster Confession addresses adiaphora in 1.6.

4   D.G. Hart, *Recovering Mother Kirk* (Eugene, Ore.: Wipf & Stock, 2003), 98.

5   Donald Whitney, "Private Worship," in *Give Praise to God: A Vision for Reforming Worship: Celebrating the Legacy of James Montgomery Boice*, eds. Philip Graham Ryken, Derek Thomas, and J. Ligon Duncan (Phillipsburg, N.J.: P&R, 2011), 312.

Chapter 5

1   Gardiner Spring, *The Power of the Pulpit* (London: Banner of Truth, 1986), 109.

2   J.I. Packer, "The Pastor as Theologian," in *When God's Voice Is Heard: Essays on Preaching Presented to Dick Lucas*, eds. Christopher Green and David Jackman (Leicester, England: InterVarsity Press, 2003).

3   R. Albert Mohler Jr., *He Is Not Silent: Preaching in a Postmodern World* (Chicago: Moody, 2008), 17.

4   John A. Broadus, *On the Preparation and Delivery of Sermons*, 4th ed, rev. by Vernon L. Stanfield (San Francisco: Harper Collins, 1979), 3. Cited by Mohler, *He Is Not Silent*, 17.

5   Mohler, *He Is Not Silent*, 21.

6   John Stott, *Guard the Truth: The Message of 1 Timothy and Titus* (Downers Grove, Ill.: InterVarsity Press, 1996), 121.

7   Broadus, *On the Preparation and Delivery of Sermons*, 165.

8   R.W. Dale, *Nine Lectures on Preaching*, vol. 2, *A.D. 1572–1900* (London: Hodder and Stoughton and G.H. Doran, 1912), 46. Cited by John R.W. Stott, *I Believe in Preaching* (London: Hodder and Stoughton, 1982), 250.

9   John E. Booty, ed., *The Book of Common Prayer, 1559* (Charlottesville, Va.: University of Virginia Press, 2005), 79.

Chapter 6

1   You may recall that in a previous chapter, we noted that there is no
    express command to keep the fourth commandment, but that did not
    lead us to conclude that there is no such requirement in the new cove-
    nant era.

2   It is sometimes referred to as "alms" and was in the past included in
    Reformed liturgies for the celebration of the Lord's Supper.

3   Paul Gardner, *1 Corinthians*, Exegetical Commentary on the New Testa-
    ment, ed. Clinton E. Arnold (Grand Rapids, Mich.: Zondervan, 2018), 25.

4   Gardner, *1 Corinthians*, 25.

5   Gardner, *1 Corinthians*, 26.

6   Hughes Oliphant Old, *The Patristic Roots of Reformed Worship* (Zurich:
    Theologischer Verlag, 1975), 39–50. Old cites the first Reformed celebra-
    tion of the Lord's Supper as occurring in the city of Memmingen, Germany,
    on December 7, 1524; an official liturgy was drawn up there in November
    1528, and it shows that the collection of alms occurred after the benedic-
    tion (see Old, *Patristic Roots*, 39n11). It is conceivable that Calvin included
    the giving of alms with the weekly celebration of the Lord's Supper (which
    he advocated), but this is nowhere made explicitly clear.

7   Westminster Confession of Faith 21.4–5. Nor does the offering appear in
    the Westminster Assembly's Directory for the Public Worship of God.

8   The term "sanctuary" is not a good one, though it is widely used. There is
    nothing "holy" about the space itself. Puritans frequently called the space
    where public worship was offered a "meeting place." Superstitions arise
    when we attach too much significance to the space itself.

9   Jon D. Payne, *The Elements of Christian Worship* (Douglasville, Ga.:
    GPC, 2007), 46.

Chapter 7

1   This version of Chrysostom's prayer can be found in Charles Mortimer
    Guilbert, ed., *The Book of Common Prayer: and Administration of the
    Sacraments and Other Rites and Ceremonies of the Church Together with
    the Psalter or Psalms of David according to the Use of the Episcopal Church*
    (New York: Church Publishing Inc., 1979), 72.

2   For some inexplicable reason, American Presbyterians typically employ
    the Matthew version with the mention of "debts" while Episcopa-
    lians employ the Luke version, which (in the KJV) employs the word

"trespasses." You can always tell the visiting Episcopalian in our own church at that point.

3   For a variety of reasons, this is difficult to do in a large congregation.

4   See Calvin, *Institutes of the Christian Religion* 1.9.3 (1:95–96).

5   Hughes Oliphant Old, *Themes & Variations for a Christian Doxology: Some Thoughts on the Theology of Worship* (Grand Rapids, Mich.: Eerdmans, 1992), 19.

6   Hughes Oliphant Old, *Worship: Reformed according to Scripture* (Louisville, Ky.: Westminster John Knox, 2002), 95.

7   The longer ending does not appear in the ESV but does in the KJV. It is found in the *Didache*, a source that is certainly second century, and some would argue that it is first century. It includes a great deal of information on early church worship. The longer ending occurs in the Byzantine family of texts going back to the fourth century and on which the KJV rests. The ESV represents the Alexandrian family. These two traditions agree on 99 percent of the text. The longer ending is one of the ways they disagree.

8   Michael Horton, *A Better Way: Rediscovering the Drama of God-Centered Worship* (Grand Rapids, Mich.: Baker, 2003), 156.

9   Samuel Miller, *Thoughts on Public Prayer* (Harrisonburg, Va.: Sprinkle, 1985), 262. Cited by R. Kent Hughes, *The Pastor's Book: A Contemporary and Practical Guide to Pastoral Ministry* (Wheaton, Ill.: Crossway, 2015), 265.

10 Hughes, *The Pastor's Book*, 265.

Chapter 8

1   We need not detain ourselves unduly with the (somewhat complicated) history of the origin and development of the Apostles' Creed. Suffice it to say that it was not written by the Apostles! The gist of it is quoted in Greek by Marcellus of Ancyra in AD 340 and in Latin by Rufinus about AD 400. In a Greek form that is recognizably similar to the Apostles' Creed, it is found in Hippolytus' *Apostolic Tradition* early in the third century. And Hippolytus' use of it implies that the Greek form exists in the second century. We can therefore trace the skeletal form of the Apostles' Creed to within a few generations of the first-century Apostles.

2   For a comprehensive treatment of the doctrine of the Trinity as well as the use of the "detective" metaphor, I would recommend Robert Letham, *The Holy Trinity: In Scripture, History, Theology, and Worship*, revised and expanded ed. (Phillipsburg, N.J.: P&R, 2019). For a more

user-friendly treatment, readers should consult Michael Reeves, *Delighting in the Trinity* (Downers Grove, Ill.: IVP Academic, 2012).

3   J.I. Packer, *Affirming the Apostles' Creed* (Wheaton, Ill.: Crossway, 2008), 86–87.

4   Wayne A. Grudem, *The First Epistle of Peter: An Introduction and Commentary*, Tyndale New Testament Commentaries 17 (Grand Rapids, Mich.: Eerdmans, 1988), 203–39.

5   Calvin, *Institutes of the Christian Religion* 2.16.8–12 (1:512–20).

6   Calvin, *Institutes of the Christian Religion* 2.16.10–11 (1:515–17).

7   Calvin, *Institutes of the Christian Religion* 3.1.1 (537).

8   J.I. Packer, *Affirming the Apostles' Creed* (Wheaton, Ill.: Crossway, 2008), 131–32.

9   John Bunyan, *The Pilgrim's Progress*, ed. Roger Pooley (London: Penguin, 2011), 41.

10 Derek W.H. Thomas, *Heaven on Earth: What the Bible Teaches about Life to Come* (Fearn, Scotland: Christian Focus, 2018), 108.

Chapter 9

1   The Colossians passage raises the issue of whether "psalms, hymns, and spiritual songs" modifies "singing" or the previous participles, "teaching and admonishing." Both are grammatically possible, and commentators, according to Douglas Moo, are equally divided. Since the Ephesian passage is clearer, "addressing one another in psalms and hymns and spiritual songs," Moo, for this and other grammatical considerations, opts for the "teaching and admonishing" participles in the Colossians passage. See Douglas Moo, *The Letters to the Colossians and to Philemon* (Grand Rapids, Mich.: Eerdmans, 2008), 287.

2   Another grammatical issue makes the interpretation a little more nuanced. Does the term "spiritual" modify only the word "songs," as the ESV suggests, or should it modify all three terms, "psalms," "hymns," and "songs"? Strictly speaking, as again Moo makes clear, the grammar suggests the ESV reading is correct. Moo, *The Letters to the Colossians and to Philemon*, 290.

3   Scot McKnight, *The Letter to the Colossians*, NICNT (Grand Rapids, Mich.: Eerdmans, 2018), 332. Old, *Worship: Reformed according to Scripture*, 39.

4   Old, *Worship: Reformed according to Scripture*, 41.

5   Old, *Worship: Reformed According to Scripture*, 39.

6   Moo, *The Letters to the Colossians and to Philemon*, 288–89.

7 Cf. Norval Geldenhuys, *Commentary on the Gospel of Luke*, NICNT (Grand Rapids, Mich.: Eerdmans, 1993), 85; Philip Graham Ryken, Derek Thomas, and J. Ligon Duncan, eds., "Hymnody in a Post-Hymnody World," in *Give Praise to God: A Vision for Reforming Worship: Celebrating the Legacy of James Montgomery Boice* (Phillipsburg, N.J.: P&R, 2011), 226–27.

8 From the Latin for "Magnify."

9 From the Latin for "Blessed."

10 From the Latin for "Glory to God in the highest."

11 From the Latin for "Now, let [Your servant] depart."

12 Psalm 90 is attributed to Moses, and Psalm 89, attributed to Ethan the Ezrahite, is postexilic.

13 See Old, *Worship: Reformed according to Scripture*, 33–36.

14 Old, *Worship: Reformed according to Scripture*, 36.

15 Lester Hostetler, *Handbook to the Mennonite Hymnary* (Newton, Kans.: General Conference of the Mennonite Church in North America, 1949), xvii. Cited by Robert E. Webber, *Worship Old and New*, rev. ed. (Grand Rapids, Mich.: Zondervan, 1994), 199.

Chapter 10

1 My understanding of baptism was fundamentally shaped by Dr. Sinclair B. Ferguson. He gave two lectures in the late 1980s at a gathering of ministers in Northern Ireland. Later, these lectures were to some extent reshaped in a chapter he wrote in *Baptism: Three Views*, ed. David F. Wright (Downers Grove, Ill.: IVP Academic, 2009), 77–111.

2 Westminster Confession of Faith 1:6.

3 By *credobaptist* I mean those who permit the baptism *only* of one who makes a credible profession of faith.

4 Westminster Confession of Faith 28:1.

5 Westminster Confession of Faith 27:1.

6 Evangelicals sometimes convey their lapse into thinking that there is something special about the water by asking if they can bring some water "from the Jordan River." This is nothing but sentimentalism, and when asked for permission, I always ask, "Did you boil it?"

7 Something that is done in some branches of Russian Orthodoxy, for example, and sadly with accounts of fatalities as a result.

8 Paedobaptists allow the baptism of an infant in the case where only one parent makes a credible profession of faith. The argument is often based

on something Paul says (in a different context) in 1 Corinthians 7:14, suggesting that in such a marriage, the children are "holy," in the sense that they have a different status from children born to entirely unbelieving parents.

9 Wright, ed., *Baptism: Three Views*, 85.

10 Wright, ed., *Baptism: Three Views*, 106.

11 Wright, ed., *Baptism: Three Views*, 106–7.

Chapter 11

1 The sacrament is known variously as "communion" (1 Cor. 10:16, KJV, translated "participation" in the ESV), "Lord's supper" (1 Cor. 11:20), "breaking of bread" (Luke 24:35; Acts 2:42, 46; 20:7; 1 Cor. 10:16, though some argue that some of these references refer to a fellowship meal rather than the sacrament), and "eucharist," from the Greek word for "thanksgiving" ("when he had given thanks, he broke it," Luke 22:19), though the term is usually associated with a "high view" of the sacrament suggesting a "real" or bodily presence of Christ in the sacrament.

2 There is some debate as to the connection between Passover and the Lord's Supper. Robert Letham, for example, argues that it is the covenant meal that lies behind the supper rather than Passover. However, most scholars argue for Passover. In that case, the bread would have been matzo, the kosher, unleavened bread served at Passover. See Robert Letham, *The Lord's Supper: Eternal Word in Broken Bread* (Phillipsburg, N.J.: P&R, 2001).

3 Calvin, *Institutes of the Christian Religion* 4.17.10 (2:1370). See also Sinclair Ferguson, *The Holy Spirit* (Downers Grove, Ill.: InterVarsity Press, 1996), 199–205.

4 Augustine, *Tractates on the Gospel of John: 55–111*, 117. John Calvin picked up on Augustine's famous term. See John Calvin, "Short Treatise on the Lord's Supper," in *John Calvin: Tracts and Letters*, ed. Henry Beveridge, vol. 2 (Edinburgh, Scotland: Banner of Truth, 2009), 190–91.

5 See Robert Robinson, "Come Thou Fount of Every Blessing," number 457 in *Trinity Hymnal* (Suwanee, Ga.: Great Commission, 1990).

6 I have written a lengthier response to this issue elsewhere. "'Not a Particle of Sound Brain': A Theological Response to Paedo-Communion," in *Children and the Lord's Supper,* eds. Guy Waters and Ligon Duncan (Fearn, Scotland: Mentor, 2011), 97–118. I once preached at a church and (without knowing this in advance) was asked to officiate at the supper at the close of the worship service. Just as I began the customary

liturgy, a family (husband, wife, and seven or eight children of varying ages, including an infant in arms) came and sat at the front on the floor beside me. As I was speaking, the father also spoke to the children and later offered the bread and wine to all of them, including the infant!

7   For a thorough treatment of early Christian practice see the two works by Joachim Jeremias: *The Origins of Infant Baptism: A Further Study in Reply to Kurt Aland* (Eugene, Ore.: Wipf & Stock, 2004) and *Infant Baptism in the First Four Centuries* (Eugene, Ore.: Wipf & Stock, 2004).

8   These were words Sinclair Ferguson almost always used at the supper at First Presbyterian Church of Columbia when he was the senior minister.

9   Robert Bruce (1551–1631) was the successor to John Knox at St. Giles, Edinburgh, Scotland. In February and March of 1589, he preached a series of five sermons on the supper, which were later published. The quotation can be found in Robert Bruce, *The Mystery of the Lord's Supper*, ed. T.F. Torrance (Edinburgh, Scotland: Christian Focus, 2005), 85.

10   Westminster Confession of Faith 28:3.

11   Charles Hodge, *Systematic Theology* (repr., Peabody, Mass.: Hendrickson, 2003), 3:523–25.

Chapter 12

1   *Grace Be with You: Benedictions from Dale Ralph Davis* (Fearn, Scotland: Christian Focus, 2018). The book contains a foreword and afterword written by me and Sinclair B. Ferguson, respectively.

2   Various Reformed traditions disagree, suggesting that the benedictions are prayers. For example, "Benedictions are not to be pronounced or 'said,' but prayed with the pastor's heart and mind fully engaged." R. Kent Hughes, *The Pastor's Book: A Comprehensive and Practical Guide to Pastoral Ministry* (Wheaton, Ill.: Crossway, 2015), 310. A similar point of view is held by Terry L. Johnson, *Leading in Worship: A Sourcebook for Presbyterian Students and Ministers Drawing upon the Biblical and Historic Forms of the Reformed Tradition* (Oak Ridge, Tenn.: The Covenant Foundation, 1996), 36n18. This view has gained a significant following in Britain, for example, and congregants typically close their eyes during the benediction, suggesting that it is a prayer rather than a pronouncement. Behind this practice lies the legitimate fear of sacerdotalism—that in pronouncing the benediction, the preacher is officiating more like a priest than a minister.

Subject Index

Scripture Index